Albert Schmitz
Edith Schmitz

TOOLBOX

ENGLISH

for
Technical Purposes

2

Teacher's Book

Max Hueber Verlag

Das Werk und seine Teile sind urheberrechtlich geschützt.
Jede Verwendung in anderen als den gesetzlich zugelassenen
Fällen bedarf deshalb der vorherigen schriftlichen
Einwilligung des Verlages.

3. 2. 1. | Die letzten Ziffern
2000 1999 98 97 96 | bezeichnen Zahl und Jahr des Druckes.
Alle Drucke dieser Auflage können, da unverändert,
nebeneinander benutzt werden.
1. Auflage
© 1996   Max Hueber Verlag, D-85737 Ismaning
Sprachliche Durchsicht und Beratung: Eileen Anne Plümer
Verlagsredaktion: Cornelia Dietz, München
Umschlaggestaltung: Alois Sigl, Ismaning
Zeichnungen: Paul Netzer, Berlin
Satz: typo spezial Ingrid Geithner, Isen
Druck und Bindung: Manz AG, Dillingen
Printed in Germany
ISBN 3–19–022417–X

Inhalt

Vorwort 4

Hinweise zu den einzelnen Units und Kopiervorlagen
1. Engineering as a career 7
2. Cars and driving: safety features 13
3. Transportation problems 18
4. Energy efficiency 22
5. An APM in action 27
6. "Conveyors International" 31
7. Aluminium extraction 35
8. Aluminium extrusion 39
9. Working with steel 43
10. Applying for a job 47

Testing Your Language – Part One 54

11. Testing and finishing (1) 55
12. Testing and finishing (2) 59
13. Plastics in daily use 63
14. The Docklands Light Railway 67
15. Cleaning the air 71
16. Working with a machining center 75
17. A helping hand (1) 80
18. A helping hand (2) 84
19. Bits and bytes: PROCEDE for Windows 88
20. Bits and bytes: Images and cyberspace 93

Testing Your Language – Part Two 99

Tapescripts der Hörverständnisübungen im *Coursebook* 100
Stichwortregister 124

Vorwort

Bestandteile von Toolbox 2

Die Units im **Coursebook** sind so gestaltet worden, daß sie den Lernenden einen Einblick in die Sprache bestimmter Fachgebiete geben, so zum Beispiel

- Automobilbau
- Transport und Verkehr
- Energie und Umwelt
- Fördertechnik
- Werkstoffe (Metalle und Kunststoffe)
- Testverfahren
- Industrieroboter / Elektronik
- Computertechnik (Programme, virtuelle Realität)

Dabei ist konsequent darauf geachtet worden, die technischen Inhalte trotz aller Fachbezogenheit allgemeinverständlich zu halten. Das bedeutet vor allem, daß jede/r technisch Interessierte die angebotenen Materialien im Coursebook verstehen kann, auch ohne ganz spezielle Fachkenntnisse auf dem gerade anstehenden Gebiet zu haben.

Zum **Coursebook** gibt es **eine Cassette** bzw. **CD** mit dem Hörverständnisteilen des **Coursebook**. Das **Workbook** wird ebenfalls von einer **Cassette** begleitet (Hörverständnisübungen, kurze Texte, Diktate).

Ergänzend dazu bietet das **Workbook** Übungen verschiedener Art – Grammatik, Hörverständnis, Texte und Präpositionen, alle mit Lösungsschlüssel im Anhang einschließlich der Tapescripts. Außerdem hat das **Workbook** eine Kurzgrammatik, eine Zusammenfassung und Ergänzung der vermittelten Grammatikbereiche.

Im **Teacher's Book** findet die Kursleiterin/der Kursleiter neben dem Lösungsschlüssel Hinweise zum Einsatz der verschiedenen Units und der einzelnen Übungsarten. Besonders hervorzuheben wären die Kopiervorlagen, die zu jeder Unit vorhanden sind. Damit kann die Kursleiterin/der Kursleiter je nach Bedarf weitere Übungen in den Unterricht einfließen lassen. Das **Teacher's Book** bietet auch viele technische Informationen und Erläuterungen, die der Kursleiterin/dem Kursleiter helfen sollen, wenn auf dem entsprechenden Gebiet spezielle Fachkenntnisse fehlen. Die Praxis hat gezeigt, daß viele Kursleiter/innen technisches Englisch unterrichten, die nicht unbedingt selbst Techniker/innen oder Ingenieur/innen sind – für diese Gruppe sind die genannten Hilfen in erster Linie gedacht.

Zum Einsatz von Toolbox 2 im Unterricht –
Bestandteile und Methodik

Leseverstehen:
Auf fortgeschrittenem Niveau nimmt die Textarbeit einen größeren Umfang ein. Daher findet man in **Toolbox 2** viele zusammenhängende Sachtexte, die auf verschiedene Weise erarbeitet werden können. Die erste Vorstellung des Textinhaltes kann bei geschlossenen Büchern erfolgen, indem die Kursleiterin/der Kursleiter eine kurze Beschreibung des Inhalts liefert. Anschließend kann eine kurze Diskussion von Nutzen sein. Als Hilfen findet man Verständnisfragen (Textfragen) und einführende (*warm-up*) Teile. Natürlich können die Texte auch in häuslicher Arbeit vorbereitet werden. Weitere Varianten der Textarbeit: Einteilung in Gruppen, Erarbeitung verschiedener Abschnitte, danach Zusammenfassung.

Diktat:
Auch Diktate haben ihre (wenn auch eingeschränkte) Funktion: sie können den Lernenden helfen, sich durch das Schreiben Vokabeln und Redewendungen besser einzuprägen. Daher ist es durchaus nützlich, in die Unterrichtsstunde ein kurzes Diktat einzuplanen.

Grammatik:
Die vorgestellten Grammatikerläuterungen dienen der Bewußtmachung des Gelernten und (in der Regel) vorher Geübten. Sie sind im allgemeinen sehr knapp gehalten und sollen nur eine Art „Gerüst" darstellen. Wichtig ist die praktische Einübung der Strukturen anhand des Übungsmaterials.

Hörverständnis:
Ein ganz wesentlicher Bestandteil sind die Hörverständnisübungen, die man in jeder Unit vorfindet. Begleitend zu den Dialogen, Diskussionen und Sachtexten auf den Tonträgern findet die Kursleiterin/der Kursleiter verschiedene Hilfen, so zum Beispiel

– *Questions on the text*

– *Note-taking*

– *Group work*

– *Memos*

– *Warm-up sections*

– *Fill-in forms*

– *True-False questions*

Schriftliche Arbeit:
Auf höherem Lernniveau gewinnen auch schriftliche Arbeiten an Bedeutung. Man findet Anleitungen zum Abfassen von Notizen, Tabellen zum Ausfüllen (zum Beispiel *job aspects*), Zusammenfassungen, Aufzeichnen einer Nachricht, Gruppenarbeit (mit Notizen) und Bewerbungsschreiben.

Kommunikative Übungsformen:
Großer Wert wurde auf Übungen gelegt, die zum Sprechen und Diskutieren anregen. Mündliche Arbeit macht den Lernerfolg am schnellsten sichtbar und wirkt stark motivierend auf die Kursteilnehmer/innen. Dazu dienen unter anderem Textverständnisfragen, Bildbeschreibungen, Wiedergabe gehörter Dialoge und kurze Diskussionen.

Wortschatz und Präpositionen:
Diese Bereiche werden durch zahlreiche Übungen abgedeckt, unter anderem Einfüll- und Definitionsübungen. Auch im Arbeitsbuch findet die/der Lernende viel Übungsmaterial zu diesem Thema.

Weiterführende und begleitende Materialien:
Von einem gewissen Stadium an ist es empfehlenswert, sogenannte „Realien" in den Unterricht einzuführen, zumindest gelegentlich. Dazu gehören technische Prospekte, Bedienungsanleitungen, technische Zeichnungen, Broschüren technischer Museen sowie teilweise Versandhauskataloge und -broschüren. Diese Materialien kann sich die Kursleiterin/der Kursleiter im Laufe der Zeit beschaffen, zum Beispiel bei einem Aufenthalt in einem englischsprechenden Land oder durch das Anschreiben von Firmen. Wenn man den Verwendungszweck beschreibt, sind Firmen in der Regel gerne bereit, Materialien zur Verfügung zu stellen.
In ähnlicher Weise lassen sich Realien anderer Art einsetzen, wie zum Beispiel englische und amerikanische Stecker und Steckdosen, Werkzeuge und (wenn man sie zur Verfügung hat) Funktionsmodelle von Motoren und Maschinen.

1 Engineering as a career

Lernstoffübersicht – Lehr- und Arbeitsbuch
Schwerpunkte

Themen / Inhalte	Grammatik / Übungen	Situations / Functions
Einführung in die verschiedenen Bezeichnungen für Ingenieurberufe Merkmale, Profile, Arbeitsbereiche	Konstruktionen mit *own* und *-self* / Besondere Ausdrücke mit *-self* (z. B. *self-contained, self-winding, self-lubricating*)	Reaktion auf berufliche Situationen (z. B. Arbeitszeit, Arbeitsplatz, Bezahlung)
Allgemeine Besprechung der beruflichen Anforderungen (z. B. Kontakt mit Kollegen und Kolleginnen)	Diskussion / *Note-taking* (*Telephone message*)	Jemand etwas versichern / etwas bestätigen (z. B. *We can assure you ... / We try to make sure ...*)

Technische Hintergrundinformationen

civil engineering: deals with the design and construction of buildings and public structures, such as roads, railways, dams, canals, etc. *(= Bauwesen, Bauingenieurwesen).*

chemical engineering: the theory and practice of designing, setting up, and operating apparatus for the large-scale manufacture of the products of chemical reactions *(= Chemische Verfahrenstechnik).*

mechanical engineering: a major branch of engineering dealing mainly with means of transport (ships, railways, motor-cars and airplanes), power generation and mechanical power transmission, and the production of machine tools *(= Maschinenbau).*

metallurgy: the branch of science which deals with the extraction of metals from their ores, the production of alloys, and the working, as well as the structure and constitution, of metals and alloys *(= Metallurgie, Hüttenwesen).*

telecommunications: the transfer of information by electromagnetic means, such as wire or radio waves; telecommunications includes telephones, telegraphy, radio, television, etc. *(= Nachrichtentechnik, Fernmeldewesen).*

process engineering = *Verfahrenstechnik*

process metallurgy = *metallurgische Verfahrenstechnik*

process model = *Prozeßmodell*

process monitoring = *Prozeßüberwachung*

craftsperson (also: artisan): a person skilled in doing something with the hands (e.g. a carpenter, plumber, or tailor) *(= Handwerker; auch: Kunsthandwerker)*.

Es lohnt sich sicher auch, die Kursteilnehmer/innen noch einmal auf folgenden Sprachgebrauch hinzuweisen:

engineering: 1) the application of scientific principles to practical ends as the design, construction, and operation of efficient and economical structures, equipment and systems *(= Technik)*; 2) the profession of or the work performed by an engineer *(=Ingenieur-wesen)*.

technique: method used in carrying out a mechanical, artistic, or scientific work: technical skill *(= Technik im Sinne von Verfahren, Methode)*.

technology: study of how to put scientific knowledge to practical use: applied science *(= Technologie)*.

Schlüssel zu den Übungen im Lehrbuch

1. Fragen zum Text *The Industry*
2. a. confirm   b. confirm   c. sure   d. assure   e. sure
3. Hörverständnisübung und *note-taking* – vergleiche Tapescript im Anhang S. 100
4. Beispiele: I plan the software, develop special programs, and service the equipment. / Mary plans the software, repairs the machines, and services the equipment. / Rudolph repairs the machines and services the equipment. / Vicky develops special programms, checks the figures, and services the equipment.
5. Diskussion zum Thema Berufsausbildung
6. Offene Kommunikationsübung zum Thema „Berufe"
7. *note-taking*
   a. FROM: John Hamilton, International Machine Tools
   TO: Lisa Miller
   DATE: (today's date)
   Milling machine she ordered left factory this morning – probable delivery tomorrow – can reach John Hamilton this afternoon (886-22971)
   b. FROM: Mary Rosewall, InterElectronics
   TO: Frank Slide
   DATE: (today's date)
   Order No. M/6-94 – cannot deliver before Monday – please call back tomorrow morning – Do you still want 20 modems?
8. Erstellen einer Vorgangsbeschreibung in Gruppenarbeit

9. Diskussion über Streßfaktoren in verschiedenen Berufen

10. a. yourself/yourselves   b. ourselves   c. themselves   d. myself   e. herself   f. themselves   g. himself   h. herself

Anmerkungen und Schlüssel zu den Kopiervorlagen

2. a. an alloy   b. ore   c. copper   d. steel   e. metals

3. a. of your own – one of my own / my own workshop   b. one of his own   c. of my own   d. one of our own / our own / our own RV

4. Beispiele:
   civil engineering: public buildings / bridges / roads / canals;
   chemical engineering: designing, setting up, and operating apparatus for large-scale manufacturing of chemical products;
   mechanical engineering: power generation and transmission / transport / machine tools;
   metallurgy: extraction of metals / alloys / working with metals / treating metals (e. g. surface coating)

5. a. 5,250 people   b. £9,750   c. £37.50

6. Beispiele:
   operate equipment / design machines and machine tools / maintain highways / install control equipment / work with metal and plastics / set up apparatus / plan plants and machines / perform various technical jobs / draw plans / analyse the performance of a machine

| Kopiervorlage | Unit 1 |

1
Zusätzlicher Text / Diktat:

The term "engineering" is a broad one which has come to mean almost any application of physical and chemical ideas to practical uses. The term may be divided into four main categories: mechanical engineering, electrical engineering, civil engineering and chemical engineering.
Mechanical engineering includes the design and building of machines, machine tools, engines of all kinds, pumps, and motor vehicles. Electrical engineers concentrate on the design, installation and maintenance of electrical devices such as generators, transformators, switches, radio and television equipment and domestic wiring. The civil engineer is responsible for building roads, railways, dams and bridges and tunnels. Another aspect of the civil engineer's work may be the erection of buildings of all kinds, though this is more usually in the hands of architects and builders. Chemical engineers are concerned with the adjustment of chemical laboratory techniques to an industrial scale.
One of the important aspects of most forms of engineering is the study of stress in materials. The engineer must know how each material will react when subjected to all kinds of stresses. In this way, the projects can be designed with the minimum of wasted material and the maximum of strength.

2
Finden Sie die richtige Antwort:

a. What do you get by mixing two or more types of metal together? _____

b. Rock or earth from which metal can be obtained is called _____.

c. Which metal ist reddish brown, soft and used for wires? _____

d. Which metal is strong, usually made from iron and is, for example, used for making bridges? _____

e. Iron, steel, lead, copper are all _____.

3
Vervollständigen Sie die untenstehenden Sätze mit einer Form von *own*:

a. Do you have a workshop _____ ? – No, unfortunately not, but I wish I had _____.

b. He always uses my wrench. Hasn't he got _____ ?

c. My computer broke down but fortunately through no fault _____.

d. So far we have always rented an RV for our holidays, but now we want _____.

Kopiervorlage   Unit 1

4
Womit haben die einzelnen Felder zu tun? Welche Arbeit wird dort geleistet? Diskutieren Sie anschließend Ihre Ergebnisse.

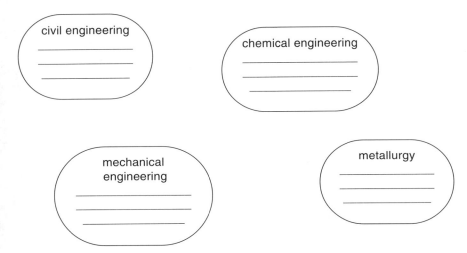

5
... and some simple maths:

a. A large company employs 15% of the working population in a small town. The total population of the town is 70,000 of which 50% is the working population. How many people are employed by the company?

b. A computer programmer earns £12,000 gross per year. She is entitled to a tax-free personal allowance of £3,000 and pays income tax at 25% on the balance. What is her net pay per year?

c. An employer has 60 people working for her and she wants to give a 15% bonus to all her staff. How much would each staff member receive if the total weekly wage bill is normally £15,000?

Kopiervorlage   Unit 1

6
Was müssen Techniker/innen und Ingenieur/innen können?
Vervollständigen Sie die untenstehenden Felder mit einem passenden Begriff:

- operate
- design
- maintain
- install
- work
- set up
- plan
- perform
- draw
- analyse

Anschließend besprechen Sie Ihre Ergebnisse und
diskutieren Sie über Ihre Tätigkeitsfelder.

2 Cars and driving: safety features

Lernstoffübersicht – Lehr- und Arbeitsbuch
Schwerpunkte

Themen / Inhalte	Grammatik / Übungen	Situations / Functions
Einführung in das Vokabular rund um die Autoreparatur (anhand eines Formulars) / Darstellung verschiedener Sicherheitseinrichtungen der Kraftfahrzeuge (z. B. Kopfstützen, Sicherheitslenkräder und Polsterungen)	Einsatz der Fragefürwörter *who, which, what,* und *whose* (mit Satzbeispielen) —— Partnerarbeit (Situation: Gespräch über Autoreparaturen) —— Telefongespräch	Verhalten am Telefon (Gespräch über Autoreparatur / mit der Werkstatt / mit Kund/innen) —— Etwas vorschlagen / Vorschläge und Ideen annehmen oder (in höflicher Form) ablehnen

Technische Hintergrundinformationen

Alexander Fleming (1881–1955): British bacteriologist; discovered penicillin.

Henry Ford (1863–1947): American automobile designer and manufacturer.

Thomas Alva Edison (1847–1931): American inventor; obtained 1,100 patents in such fields as telegraphy, phonography, electric lighting, and photography.

Armaturenbrett (auch: Instrumententafel) = 1) dashboard; 2) facia (also: fascia) ['fɛɪʃə] (GB); 3) instrument panel; 4) instrument board; 5) instrument facia (GB)

Schlüssel zu den Übungen im Lehrbuch

1. Hörverständnisübung:

    Message A
        Caller's name: ___Luke Taylor___
        Caller's company: ___Exec International___
        Reason for call: ___wants to talk to___
        ___Mr Roberts___
        Number of caller: ___639 4427___
        Who will call back? ___Mr Roberts___

Message B

　　　Caller's name: __Adam Jonson__
　　　Caller's company: _Buckland Motors Limited_
　　　Who does the caller want to speak to? _Michael Jones_
　　　Reason for call: __problems with spreadsheets__
　　　_____(spreadsheet 663)_____
　　　Who will help the caller: _John Davies – will fax the_
　　　_____spreadsheet to Adam Jonson right away__

2. I really don't think that's such a good idea. / Let's use the laser printer, shall we? / Shall I call her office? – That would be a good idea. / We might as well wait here – I think she'll be down in a minute. / What about a short walk to the new plant? / What about a drink at the pub? – I'd rather not – I'm driving today. / You can sit down here if you like.

3. Fragen zu *"Early Bird" Repair Order* und Diskussion

4. Diskussion über Fragen zur Sicherheit bei Kraftfahrzeugen und im Straßenverkehr.

5. a. True　b. False　c. False (the central pad is impact-absorbent)　d. False

6. Who was a famous American inventor and manufacturer? = Henry Ford / Who invented the electric light bulb? = Thomas Alva Edison / Which (What) is colder – the North Pole or the South Pole? = The South Pole / What is the oldest parliament in the British Isles? = Number 10 Dowing Street / What is our closest neighbour in space? = The Moon / Who discovered penicillin? = Alexander Fleming

7. Mögliche Antworten:
a. the steel cage b. it is designed to absorb collision forces and protect the interior c. sturdy, protective steel members in the doors d. one at the front and one at the rear e. it is a safe location f. it has a lining of flame-resistant, moulded glass fibre and reinforcing members in the roof structure g. there are seat belts for all occupants h. they have "anti-submarining" protection i. to protect the driver in an accident j. it absorbs the impact in case of a collision k. head restraints / crumple zones

8. a. at　b. to　c. to　d. with　e. for　f. on　g. with　h. of　i. in

9. Dialoge: sich beschweren und auf eine Beschwerde reagieren

10. Hörverständnisübung – vergleiche Tapescript im Anhang S. 102

11. Diskussion über Vor- und Nachteile von Arbeitsplätzen im Büro gegenüber einer Fabrik.

Anmerkungen und Schlüssel zu den Kopiervorlagen

2., 3. und 4. sind offene Kommunikationsübungen; zusätzliche Vokabelerläuterungen:

dash brake light = *Bremslichtanzeige am Armaturenbrett*

bled (von bleed) = *entlüftet*

flush = *ausspülen*

seem to be dragging = *zu schleifen scheinen*

lock at times = *manchmal blockieren*

grab = *greifen*

chatter = *flattern*

pulsate = *eine pulsierende Bewegung machen*

spongy = *schwammig*

Kopiervorlage — Unit 2

1
Zusätzlicher Text / Diktat:

Alignment has to do with the angle, made by the suspension components, at which the car's wheels meet the road. It is a compromise angle, because to get the most out of their treads, your tires would like to roll absolutely straight down the road. This position would maximize their useful lives. But a straight relationship to the road does not promote good road handling. The car would feel heavy and unresponsive as it went through turns. For the car to handle well, the tires need to sit slightly off the vertical, slightly tilted to the road surface. If you want to get the most out of a set of tires, have an alignment done at least once a year. The frequency of alignment depends on the type of driving you do and the road conditions.

2
Kundenbefragung
Pair Work. Zwei Kursteilnehmer/innen entwickeln je ein Telefongespräch.

Eine Kursteilnehmerin/ein Kursteilnehmer hat ihr/sein Auto von der Inspektion abgeholt. Es waren mehrere Reparaturarbeiten angefallen.
Ein paar Tage später wird der Kunde/die Kundin von der Werkstatt angerufen. Man fragt nach, ob er/sie mit dem Service zufrieden war.
Untenstehend finden Sie einige Ausdrücke, die Sie in das Gespräch integrieren können.

Oxford Car Care Centre	Kundin/Kunde
Satisfied with service?	Well, _____
Car running smoothly now?	As a matter of fact _____
Satisfied with price charged?	Well, you know _____
Waited on promptly?	I tell you what _____
Personnel friendly and informative?	No way _____
Service performed in a reasonable amount of time?	Ah, well _____
Will return to workshop?	

Kopiervorlage   **Unit 2**

Oxford Car Care Centre

BRAKE SYMPTOMS CHECKLIST

Help our technicians help you.

1. Does your car stop OK?
   - _____ Yes
   - _____ No
   - _____ Sometimes

2. The brake pedal seems:
   - _____ To work OK
   - _____ Hard
   - _____ Soft
   - _____ Too high
   - _____ Too low
   - _____ Spongy
   - _____ To pulsate or chatter
   - _____ To work better when pumped
   - _____ To return too slowly

3. The car:
   - _____ Stops straight
   - _____ **Always** pulls in one direction
   - _____ Pulls left only when braking
   - _____ Pulls right only when braking

4. The brakes:
   - _____ Grab
   - _____ Lock at times
   - _____ Seem to be dragging
   - _____ Make noise

   Describe noise _____

5. The Emergency/Park Brake:
   - _____ Is seldom used
   - _____ Works OK
   - _____ Doesn't work properly

   Explain _____

6. Has brake fluid been added in the last 6 months?
   - _____ Yes
   - _____ No

7. Have the brakes been flushed and bled in the last 6 months?   Adjusted?
   - _____ Yes   _____ Yes
   - _____ No   _____ No

8. Is dash brake light on?
   - _____ Yes
   - _____ No

9. Last time brakes were serviced or repaired:
   - _____ 3 Months
   - _____ 6 Months
   - _____ 1 Year
   - _____ Longer

10. Other problems: _____
    _____
    _____
    _____

3
Besprechen Sie die Checkliste und füllen Sie sie aus.

4
Pair Work
Ein Kursteilnehmer/eine Kursteilnehmerin ist Mechaniker/in beim *Oxford Car Care Centre* und ein anderer Kursteilnehmer/eine andere Kursteilnehmerin ist dort Kunde/Kundin und bespricht die Checkliste mit dem „Mechaniker". Beide besprechen, was mit dem Wagen gemacht werden soll und einigen sich auf den Preis.

3 Transportation problems

Lernstoffübersicht – Lehr- und Arbeitsbuch
Schwerpunkte

Themen / Inhalte	Grammatik / Übungen	Situations / Functions
Moderne Transportsysteme, hier besonders Magnetschwebebahnen – technische Konzeption, Konstruktionsmerkmale, Einsatzmöglichkeiten	Anwendung der Relativpronomen *(who, which und whose)*, mit Beispielsätzen und Erläuterungen	Diskussionssituation (Vor- und Nachteile verschiedener Transportsysteme) / Schreiben eines Briefes
	Strukturübungen	
	Leseverstehen	Verschiedene Formen der Fragestellung (z. B. *I wonder if ...*)
Abfassen von Protokollen	Vokabelübungen	

Technische Hintergrundinformationen

<u>magnetic levitation:</u> a method of opposing the force of gravity using the mutual repulsion between two like magnetic poles *(= Magnetschwebetechnik).*

<u>permanent magnet:</u> a ferromagnetic body which retains part of the magnetization after excitation has stopped; cobalt steel, ceramic materials and ferritic alloys are often used in loudspeakers, relays, motors, and magnetrons *(= Magnetrons, Magnetfeldröhren – werden z. B. in Mikrowellengeräten verwendet) (= Dauermagnet).*

<u>linear motor:</u> a type of induction motor in which the "rotor" travels along a rail that acts as the stator.

Schlüssel zu den Übungen im Lehrbuch

1. Mögliche Antworten: a. Japan – a lot of mountains, population concentrations   b. no, it isn't, it's a monorail train   c. several countries, e.g. companies in Europe, the USA, and Japan   d. high speed, economical travel   e. no, there are several different systems   f. permanent magnets   g. they will have to be solved first

2. Hörverständnisübung – vergleiche Tapescript im Anhang S. 102

3. a. True   b. False   c. True   d. True   e. True   f. True   g. False

4. a. in ... for   b. on   c. on   d. on   e. on   f. at   g. up   h. for   i. for   j. up   k. up   l. in   m. for   n. for ... for

5. Gespräch über verschiedene Verkehrssysteme

6. a. Whose office is this? – I think it's Ms Penrose's. b. Whose idea is this? – I think it's John's. c. Whose suggestion is this? – I think it's Mr Hamilton's. d. Whose cup of coffee is this? – I think it's mine. e. Whose seat is this? – I think it's the receptionist's. f. Whose printer is this? – I think it's our chief engineer's. g. Whose car is this? – I think it's my neighbour's. h. Whose pen is this? – I think it's my colleague's. i. Whose dictionary is this? – I think it's Helen's. j. Whose bag is this? – I think it's Michael's.

7. a. Mr Smith, who was in London last Monday, works with computers. b. The engineer who introduced the new system at the conference speaks Japanese. c. The paper machine which broke down two days ago cost a lot of money. d. The technicians who installed the unit Tuesday last week are interested in the new software.

8. a. about / on   b. on   c. about

9. a. caused   b. kept   c. keep   d. keep   e. caused

10. Brief an einen Freund / eine Freundin zum Thema Verkehrssituation

Anmerkungen und Schlüssel zu den Kopiervorlagen

2. a. I wonder if you'd mind turning the heating down a little bit. b. ... opening the window. c. ... switching off the cassette recorder. d. ... eating a little less noisily e. ... smoking in the corridor.

3. a. rust   b. changeable   c. condense

4. a. magnet   b. linear   c. data   d. steam   e. handsaw   f. area   g. guideway; Endbuchstaben vertikal: tramway

| Kopiervorlage | Unit 3 |

1
Zusätzlicher Text / Diktat:

One of the latest versions of the maglev train is the MLU designed by a Japanese company. Sleek and aerodynamic, the MLU will also be luxurious, with a TV set for every passenger. There will also be a comfortable lounge, and a monitor room fitted with computers, telephones, and other equipment.
The MLU is fitted with eight electromagnets to every coach. At rest, the train sits on wheels, but as it begins to move, the electromagnets induce currents in coils mounted on the floor of the guideway. These currents produce magnetic fields which lift the train off its wheels and support it. Propulsion is provided by coils set in the side of the guideway, which re-peatedly reverse polarity, to push and pull it along.
The high-power, superconducting magnets, mounted on the train itself, are responsible for inducing opposing currents in the coils on the guideway. When the current is flowing around both sets of coils, they repel each other, lifting the train by between 10 and 20 cm. This generous clearance makes building the guideway easier. A question mark remains over whether the powerful magnets will have any health effects on passengers, and how high the costs of the track are likely to be.

2
Sie sitzen im Zug und ein paar Dinge um Sie herum stören Sie. Sie wollen das ändern, dabei aber sehr höflich sein.
Ändern Sie die Fragen nach folgendem Muster um:

<u>Statt:</u> Could you please close the window?
<u>Sagen Sie:</u> I wonder if (oder: whether) you'd mind closing the window.

a. Could you please turn down the heating a little bit?
_____

b. Could you please open the window?
_____

c. Could you please switch off the cassette recorder?
_____

d. Could you please eat a little less noisily?
_____

e. Could you please smoke in the corridor?
_____

Kopiervorlage — Unit 3

3
... and a short test with technical vocabulary:

a. Which of the following verbs means the same as "corrode"?
   correspond / corrupt / insulate / protect / rust

b. Which of the following adjectives means the same as "variable"?
   changeable / constant / stable / steady / striped

c. Which of the following verbs means the same as "compress"?
   condense / expand / impress / pressure / spread

4
Puzzle:
Finden Sie das richtige Wort. Die Endbuchstaben ergeben von oben nach unten gelesen das Wort für ein Nahverkehrsmittel.

a.
b.
c.
d.
e.
f.
g.

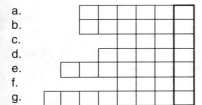

a. Piece of iron which attracts iron or steel.

b. The motor mentioned in Unit 3 which uses magnetic force to propel the train is called a _____ motor.

c. Another word for "information" which is usually in form of facts or statistics that can be analysed.

d. Something that can be seen when water boils.

e. A tool for cutting material which has a blade with sharp teeth.

f. The square metre (m²) is the SI unit of _____.

g. In Unit 3 the text tells us that the carriages are pulled above the _____ by the force of attraction.

4 Energy efficiency

Lernstoffübersicht – Lehr- und Arbeitsbuch
Schwerpunkte

Themen / Inhalte	Grammatik / Übungen	Situations / Functions
Effiziente Verwendung von Energie, hier besonders im Haus und in der Wohnung / Isolationsprobleme in Haus und Wohnung, Einsatz der verschiedenen Isolationsmaterialien	Wortkombinationen mit -ever (however, whatever, whichever, etc.)	Dialogsituation (Hörverständnis) mit kurzen technischen Erläuterungen
	Diskussion über sinnvolle Energiesparmaßnahmen im Haus oder in der Wohnung	Ausdruck des Sachverhalts „Möglichkeit" oder „Fähigkeit" (z. B. quite possible / that's a possibility)
Technische Zeichnungen	Grammatikübungen	

Technische Hintergrundinformationen

radiator: 1) a device for heating a room; a radiator is made of a series of pipes through which steam or hot water passes (= Heizkörper); 2) a device for cooling something, as an automobile engine; it usually consists of a honeycomb tank where water from the cooling system is cooled by the air (= Kühler).

mineral fibre: any inorganic fibrous material produced by steam blasting and cooling molten silicate or a similar substance; it is used as an insulator and filtering medium (= Mineralfaser).

neoprene: a synthetic rubber produced by polymerization of chloroprene and used in weather-resistant products, adhesives, shoe soles, paints, and rocket fuel (= Neopren).

Die folgenden Erläuterungen geben einen Einblick in die Wortverbindungen rund um den Begriff „Dichtung":

Abdichtung, Verschluß = seal, sealing ("an airtight closure")

Packung = packing ("a material used to prevent leakage or seepage, as around a pipe joint")

Dichtungsmanschetten = gaskets ("a layer of material placed between contact surfaces or parts needing a sealed joint; the material can be thin copper sheets, rubber, or plastic")

Dichtungsscheibe = washer ("a small perforated disk of metal, rubber, leather, or plastic, placed beneath a nut or at axle bearing or joint to relieve friction, prevent leakage, or distribute pressure")

Schlüssel zu den Übungen im Lehrbuch

1. Gespräch über Energieverbrauch in privaten Haushalten
2. a. Whatever b. whatever c. whatever d. Whoever e. However
3. a. gasket b. neoprene
4. Hörverständnisübung – vergleiche Tapescript im Anhang S. 103
5. a. she may be a bit late b. could be a bit difficult c. I can assure you d. quite impossible
6. Hörverständnisübung – vergleiche Tapescript im Anhang S. 103

Anmerkungen und Schlüssel zu den Kopiervorlagen

2. Beispiele:
   ventilation / windows that fit badly / gaps around windows and roof hatches / gaps around pipes and ducts / cracks in the ceiling
3. b. Which car are you (we) going to buy? c. Who phoned him for an appointment? d. When is she going to use the new software? e. Who do these tools belong to? f. Whose computer have you used for your work? g. What does the CAD design include? h. What can be stored and used as a fuel? i. What do you need every day? j. When did you see him? k. What is always very difficult? l. Where is his daughter studying?
4. If there is a poor leaking roof finish or a defective ceiling, there is the opportunity to add insulation as part of the repair work. / When a complete new heating system is to be installed, there is the opportunity to select a modern, efficient boiler together with effective thermostatic control. / Where existing window frames are replaced, there is the opportunity to install new ones with built-in draughtseals and double glazing.

Kopiervorlage — Unit 4

1
Zusätzlicher Text / Diktat:

Potentially, the sun could provide an almost unlimited supply of energy. The total energy needs of the United States could be met by capturing the solar energy that falls on the area covered by its roads alone.
Direct use of solar energy comes in two forms: heat, used to warm water or raise steam, and light, which can be converted directly into electricity by photovoltaic cells. Both these technologies have made progress in the past twenty years. Today, solar energy is ready to become a major source in many countries. Research into more efficient ways of using the Sun's energy is helping to bring costs down.
Solar energy has many advantages – it produces power with no pollution, and solar cells can provide power to remote places. Many villages in developing countries now rely on solar energy for power. The electricity made by solar cells can be used to split water into hydrogen and oxygen. The hydrogen can then be stored and used as a fuel.

generated

2
Wortfelder (Gruppenarbeit)

Jede Gruppe versucht, die leeren Felder mit einem passenden Begriff aus dem Wortfeldbereich zu füllen. Anschließend vergleichen die einzelnen Gruppen ihre Ergebnisse

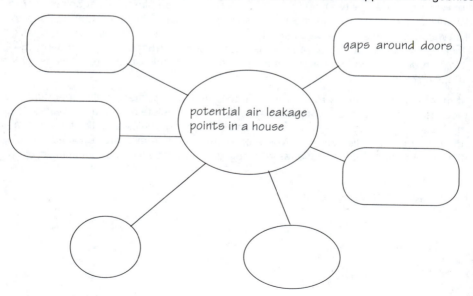

Kopiervorlage — **Unit 4**

3
Ask questions with *what, when, which, who* or *whose* (the first sentence has been done for you):

a. John's car has broken down. (whose) –
   Whose car has broken down?

b. We are going to buy the old car. (which)

c. Audrey Bell phoned him for an appointment. (who)

d. She's going to use the new software today. (when)

e. These tools belong to us. (who)

f. I've used Mary's computer for my work. (whose)

g. The CAD design includes effective crumple zones. (what)

h. Hydrogen can be stored and used as a fuel. (what)

i. I need my dictionary every day. (what)

j. I saw him in London a week ago. (when)

k. It's always very difficult to get a parking space near our house in the evening. (what)

l. His daughter is studying in Birmingham. (where)

| Kopiervorlage | | Unit 4 |

4
Bilden Sie sinnvolle Sätze, indem Sie jeweils einen Teil von A, den Teil B und einen Teil von C nehmen.

A	B	C
If there is a poor leaking roof finish or a defective ceiling ...	there is the opportunity to	... install new ones with built-in draughtseals and double glazing.
When a complete new heating system is to be installed ...		... select a modern, efficient boiler together with effective thermostatic control
Where existing window frames are replaced ...		... add insulation as part of the repair work.

5 An APM in action

Lernstoffübersicht – Lehr- und Arbeitsbuch
Schwerpunkte

Themen / Inhalte	Grammatik / Übungen	Situations / Functions
Funktionsweise, Bestandteile und Einsatzbereiche eines Zahlautomaten, mit Zeichnungen / Erklärung einiger Einzelteile des Zahlautomaten, z. B. Tastatur zur Bedienung des Menüs und zur Eingabe von Daten *(Display screen)*	Ausdrücke mit *go* (z. B. *go over something*)	Erarbeitung eines Sachtextes über Zahlautomaten (mit entsprechenden Ausdrücken und technischen Zeichnungen)
	Note-taking	
	Partnerarbeit Hörverständnis	Verschiedene Ausdrücke für den Sachverhalt „Vergleiche ziehen" (z. B. *similar to*)
	Grammatikübungen *(go)*	

Technische Hintergrundinformationen

Liquid crystal display: a digital display that consists of two sheets of glass separated by a sealed-in, normally transparent, liquid crystal material; the outer surface of each glass sheet has a transparent conductive coating such as tin oxide or indium oxide, with the viewing-side coating etched into character-forming segments that have leads going to the edges of the display; a voltage applied between front and back electrode coating disrupts the orderly arrangements of the molecules, darkening the liquid enough to form visible characters even though no light is generated *(= Flüssigkristallanzeige)*.

Schlüssel zu den Übungen im Lehrbuch

1. *note-taking*
   Mögliche Antworten: the machine can make it easier for you to pay ... / it can be used for paying local taxes, charges, rents, tickets / it accepts coins, notes, and cheques / it is easy to start – just insert a special card

2. a. are going for / go for   b. goes   c. go on   d. went out   e. goes off ... go down
   f. goes   g. go   h. go   i. go   j. go over

3. Gespräch über *APMs*

4. a. True   b. False   c. True   d. False

Anmerkungen und Schlüssel zu den Kopiervorlagen

2. Beispiele in der Reihenfolge der A-Gruppe:
   cash centre / community charge / digital display / display screen / emergency service / energy performance / key pad / service centre
3. a. $\frac{1}{60}$ hour or one minute b. 2,009.6 ft³ c. $15,691.21
4. a. Nun, ich habe meinen Schraubendreher auf dem Tisch liegen lassen und im nächsten Moment war er weg. – *2. be no longer there*
   b. Haben Sie je daran gedacht, in die Technik einzusteigen? – *4. decide to do it as your career*
   c. Wie lief die Konferenz heute? – *5. how something passes*
   d. Die Maschine lief noch, als wir in die Werkstatt gingen. – *1. be in operation*
   e. Ich fürchte, die Batterien sind leer. – *6. they no longer work*
   f. Sie werden das Projekt durchführen. – *3. begin to do something*

Kopiervorlage — Unit 5

1
Zusätzlicher Text / Diktat:

Our APMs can form part of a complete cash receipting system. Over 20 remotely sited units may be linked via modems to a central PC based control unit that will collect and process transaction and management data. By the use of a simple file transfer facility, transaction records can be transferred to any make of mainframe computer for incorporation and final account processing. Changes and additions to the accounts payable and receipt data are easily reprogrammable from the PC. Back-up systems prevent the loss of data in the event of power cuts and protect against data corruption and accidental loss or erasure of records.

The plastic account card operates in a similar manner to the way a bank or credit card operates a cash dispenser. When the card is inserted into the APM, identification data is read off the magnetic strip and the machine opened for operation. As a reminder to customers, the screen asks for the card to be removed before a receipt is issued. Invalid cards are returned to the user.

2
Group Work

Verbinden Sie ein Wort aus der A-Gruppe mit einem Wort aus der B-Gruppe, so daß ein sinnvoller Begriff entsteht. Es gibt verschiedene Kombinationsmöglichkeiten. Vergleichen Sie anschließend, welche Gruppe die meisten gefunden hat.

A	B
cash	centre
community	charge
digital	collection
display	display
emergency	screen
energy	service
key	pad
service	performance

3
... and some simple maths:

a. A falcon sees a sparrow three miles away. If the falcon's average speed is 180 miles per hour during the attack, how long will it take for the falcon to reach the sparrow?

b. A zoo in England is building a glass cylindrical tank for the small sharks. The tank is 10 feet high and has a diameter of 16 feet. How much water is needed to fill the tank (in cubic feet). (A little help: the volume of a right circular cylinder is $V = \pi r^2 h$, where r is the radius, h is the height, and $\pi \approx 3.14$).

c. A company had a loss of $1,002.91 in the first quarter, a loss of $565.77 in the second quarter, a profit of $14,232.01 in the third quarter, and a profit of $3,027.88 in the fourth quarter. What was its profit for the year?

4
Übersetzungsübung. Übersetzen Sie die untenstehenden Sätze ins Deutsche.

a. Well, I left my screwdriver on the table and the next moment is was (had) gone.

_____

b. Have you ever thought of going into engineering?

_____

c. How did the conference go today?

_____

d. The machine was still going when we went into the workshop.

_____

e. I'm afraid the batteries must have gone.

_____

f. They're going ahead with the project.

_____

In den obigen Sätzen kommen verschiedene Bedeutungen von *go* vor. Ordnen Sie diesen Sätzen nun die untenstehenden Bedeutungen von *go* zu.

1. be in operation / 2. be no longer there / 3. begin to do something / 4. decide to do it as your career / 5. how something passes / 6. they no longer work

6 "Conveyors International"

Lernstoffübersicht – Lehr- und Arbeitsbuch
Schwerpunkte

Themen / Inhalte	Grammatik / Übungen	Situations / Functions
Einführung in die Fördertechnik (hier: innerbetrieblicher Materialtransport), speziell Power-and-Free-Förderer	Ausdrücke mit *get* (z. B. *get it repaired* / *get to see*)	Einarbeitung in eine technische Zeichnung / Erarbeiten eines Textes zum Thema Förderer
Schematische Darstellung eines Förderers an zwei Beispielen (Fabriken)	Schriftliche Übung (Hinterlassen einer Nachricht – zwei Beispiele)	Schlüsse ziehen / Folgerungen aufstellen (z. B. *These are the main conclusions ...*)
	Hör- und Leseverstehen, Textfragen	

Technische Hintergrundinformationen

<u>dedicated:</u> given over to a particular purpose *(= zweckbestimmt, dediziert).*

<u>dedicated computer:</u> one which is permanently assigned to one application *(= Spezialrechner).*

<u>electrophoretic coating:</u> a surface coating on a metal deposited by an electric discharge of particles *(= elektrophoretische Beschichtung).*

Schlüssel zu den Übungen im Lehrbuch

1. Text a = drawing 2 (Paint Plant); Text b = drawing 1
2. Fragen zum Text *Conveyors International*
3. Schriftliches Erstellen einer Nachricht
4. A = b; B = b; C = a
5. a. get   b. got   c. get   d. got   e. get   f. get   g. get   h. got   i. got
6. a. do   b. decrease   c. prove   d. plan   e. come   f. do   g. come
7. a. onto   b. into   c. into   d. into

Anmerkungen und Schlüssel zu den Kopiervorlagen

2. a. Yes
   b. 15 ft per second / in 120 seconds (speed = rate at which an object moves, expressed as the distance travelled in a given time; it is measured in units such as km/h or mph; unlike velocity, it is independent of the direction of travel; speed is a scalar quantity [= Skalargröße], velocity is a vector
   c. 115,640,000 ft^3
   d. $150

3. Beispiele:
   seat assembly / dedicated manufacturing cells / gangway / paint plant / finished goods dispatch area / trim shop / stoving oven

4. Offene Kommunikationsübung

Kopiervorlage   Unit 6

1
Zusätzlicher Text / Diktat:

Conveyors International Ltd. has expanded its premises on the Troon Industrial Estate, Leicester, by some 8,000 ft² with the acquisition of an adjacent factory unit.
This means that the company can increase both manufacturing and administration areas to cope with growing demand for its products from home and overseas. As this latest issue of 'News from CI' illustrates, the company's overhead conveyors are used in the manufacture of an extensive variety of industrial and consumer products, including domestic appliances, computer housing, clothing and foodstuffs.
In particular, the extended manufacturing area will allow CI to increase the production of its popular "System 30" light duty overhead conveyor (which handles unit loads of up to 27 Kg) and adopt a more competitive pricing policy.
Formed 5 years ago, Conveyors International now has a turnover approaching £2 million and a 45-strong workforce, which it expects to increase by at least 10 this year. The company is very supportive of local youth employment schemes and works closely with the industrial Training Board and the Leicester Engineering Training Group. It is anticipated that some of the new people will come from these sources.

2
... and some simple maths:

a. A school class is going on a bus trip to an amusement park in Florida. The park requires groups to have one adult for every eight children. There are three teachers, two parents, and 36 children planning to go on the trip. Are there enough adults to meet the park's requirements?

b. A parachutist is falling from a height of 1,800 feet at a rate of 15 feet per second. Find the velocity and speed of the parachutist. When will the parachutist land on the ground?

c. The world's largest pyramid was built by the Aztec Indians in Cholula, Mexiko. It was 177 feet tall, and each side of its square base measured 1,400 feet. What was the volume of this pyramid? (A little help: the volume of a pyramid is $\frac{1}{3}$ hb, where h is the height and b is the area of the base)

d. Three computers need different circuit boards replaced on each one. The cost is $125, $150 and $175. What is the average cost per board?

Kopiervorlage   Unit 6

3
Wortfelder (Gruppenarbeit)

Jede Gruppe versucht, die leeren Felder mit einem passenden Begriff aus dem Wortfeldbereich zu füllen. Anschließend vergleichen die einzelnen Gruppen ihre Ergebnisse. Was gehört alles zu solch einer Anlage?

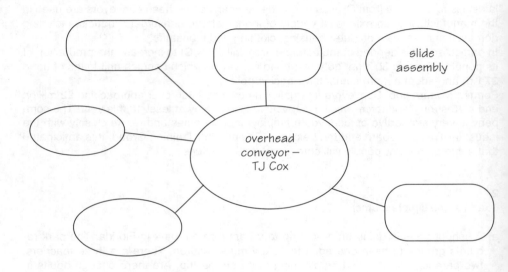

4
Telefongespräch plus Hinterlassen einer Nachricht

A. Pair Work
Arbeiten Sie folgendes Telefongespräch aus:

Eine Kollegin/ein Kollege hat Ersatzteile für eine defekte Maschine bestellt. Während sie/er in der Mittagspause ist, nehmen Sie einen Anruf von der Firma entgegen, bei der die Ersatzteile bestellt wurden. Man teilt Ihnen mit, daß Sie sich noch ein wenig gedulden müssen, da die Ersatzteile noch nicht lieferbar sind, wahrscheinlich erst in ca. 14 Tagen.

Spielen Sie das Telefongespräch durch. Machen Sie sich Notizen.

B. Hinterlassen einer Nachricht
Schreiben Sie eine Notiz über das obige Telefongespräch für Ihre Kollegin/Ihren Kollegen auf.

7 Aluminium extraction

Lernstoffübersicht – Lehr- und Arbeitsbuch
Schwerpunkte

Themen / Inhalte	Grammatik / Übungen	Situations / Functions
Kurze Beschreibung der Gewinnung von Aluminium aus Bauxit – Bestandteile, Prozesse, Resultate	Einführung in das Problem *use(d) to* – Gebrauch als Vergangenheit im Sinne von „früher ..." und als „sich gewöhnen an etwas"	Erarbeitung eines kurzen Sachtextes (mit anschließenden Fragen zum Verständnis des Textes)
Einführung in chemische Begriffe, die bei der Gewinnung von Aluminium aus Bauxit wichtig sind.	*Note-taking* und Partnerarbeit (Hörverständnis)	Ausdrücken von Gefühlen, hier besonders Zustimmung oder Ablehnung (z. B. *I do like ...*)

Technische Hintergrundinformationen

<u>aluminium:</u> aluminium oxide (Al_2O_3); it is used as an abrasive and as a structural ceramic (= *Aluminiumoxid, Tonerde*).

<u>alumina trihydrate:</u> $Al_2O_3 \cdot 3H_2O$; it is used as a fire-retarding additive in plastics (= *Aluminiumtrihydroxid*).

<u>bauxite:</u> the principal ore from which the metal aluminium is derived; it is a clay-like substance, ranging in colour from off-white to a reddish-brown; the reddish hue is caused by the presence of iron oxide; uses, apart from the productions of aluminium, include making furnace bricks, refining petroleum, and making certain chemical-resisting cements (= *Bauxit*).

<u>caustic soda:</u> this chemical compound is made up from the elements sodium, hydrogen and oxygen; its proper name is sodium hydroxide; caustic soda is a white solid, but slowly dissolves in the moisture it absorbs from the air; caustic soda is an important chemical, used in making rayon *(= Viskosefilament, Reyon)*, textiles, soap, paper, and in refining petroleum; it acts on animal and vegetable substances, especially when it is hot, and makes them soluble in water; it breaks down greases and fats (= *Natriumhydroxid, Ätznatron*).

<u>cryolite:</u> a mineral composed of sodium, aluminium, and fluorine (Na_3AlF_6) (= *Natriumfluoroaluminat, Kryolith*).

titanium: this metallic element is number 22 in the periodic table; it is obtained from the ores rutile *(= Rutil)* and ilmenite *(= Ilmenit, Titaneisenerz)*, both of which occur in the United States; pure titanium is a light, strong, corrosion-resistant metal; it is used in making light stainless steels; titanium dioxide is used in the manufacture of paints to give high covering power, and in enamels and papers as a white pigment; titanium car-bide is a very hard material used for making high-speed cutting tools *(= Titan, Titanium)*.

Schlüssel zu den Übungen im Lehrbuch

1. a. oxides of iron, silicon and titanium. b. by crushing the bauxite and dissolving it in a hot solution of caustic soda c. a sodium aluminate solution, which is then decomposed into pure alumina trihydrate and caustic soda; the trihydrate is then passed through high temperature rotary kilns d. between 950° and 1,000° C. e. a high DC current of 40 to 80 kA at low voltage f. aluminium and oxygen g. it sinks to the bottom of the cell.
2. 1 = a; 2 = b; 3 = b
3. Hörverständnisübung und *note-taking* – vergleiche Tapescript im Anhang S. 105
4. a. used   b. use   c. use   d. used   e. used   f. used   g. used
5. Hörverständnisübung und *note-taking* – vergleiche Tapescript im Anhang S. 105
6. Mögliche Antworten:
   a. I'm sorry but I wonder if you'd mind not smoking here. b. Don't you think we should have a short break now? c. I'm sorry but I'm not sure I've got all the details.

TWO GEAR WHEELS:
Both gears go back to their initial position when the wheel with 18 teeth rotates 17 times and the other wheel rotates 18 times.

Anmerkungen und Schlüssel zu den Kopiervorlagen

2. Weitere Beispiele:
   When I started work in this company, I used to put in extra hours every week. / Last year we used to sell a lot of machines to Belgium.
3. bauxite = 5.   nitrogen =1.   oxygen = 3.   silicon = 2.   titanium = 4.

1
Zusätzlicher Text / Diktat

Making aluminium – the basic processes for making aluminium cans.

Mining – Bauxite, the ore from which most aluminium is produced, is mined in a variety of sites around the world, including Guinea, Brazil, Jamaica, Suriname and Australia.

Refining – The refining process removes impurities from bauxite, leaving a pure intermediate ore called alumina – aluminium oxide.

Smelting – The powerfully bound alumina molecule is broken apart by a powerful electric currrent in the smelting process. Here, powdery alumina is converted into pure molten aluminium.

Ingot – The molten aluminium is mixed with other ingredients and cast into solid ingot forms which are then further rolled into sheet.

Rolling – Large slab ingots are reduced in thickness by rolling mills. The sheet created in this process is coiled onto spools. These coils can weigh up to 25,000 pounds.

Fabricating – Before a coil of sheet is shipped to a manufacturer, the metal must be trimmed to a specific width, leveled, cleaned, lubricated, and coated.

smelting = *Schmelzen*
ingot = *Ingot, Barren; Gußblock*
slab ingot = *Plattenbarren*
rolling mill = *Walzwerk*
coil = *Rolle, Spule*
spool = *Aufwickeltrommel*
coil of sheet = *Blechspule*
trim = *(auf Maß) schneiden; beschneiden*
level = *richten*

Kopiervorlage — Unit 7

2
Bilden Sie Sätze nach folgendem Muster:

> Eight years ago we used to work very hard in our factory.

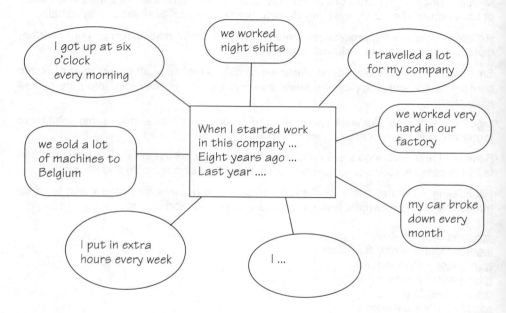

3
Welche Erklärung paßt zu welchem Wort?

a. bauxite

b. nitrogen

c. oxygen

d. silicon

e. titanium

1. colourless element that has no smell; it usually occurs as a gas

2. element that is used to make e.g. parts of computers

3. gas which is colourless; it's in the air which we all breathe

4. strong white metal used in making lightweight alloys for machine parts

5. substance from which aluminium is obtained

8 Aluminium extrusion

Lernstoffübersicht – Lehr- und Arbeitsbuch
Schwerpunkte

Themen / Inhalte	Grammatik / Übungen	Situations / Functions
Einführung in die Verarbeitung von Aluminium (hier besonders *extrusion* = Strangpressen) mit einer vereinfachten Zeichnung einer Presse	Verwendung der Ausdrücke *double, half, quite, such* und *twice* (mit Beispielen)	Arbeit in der Gruppe (Hörverständnis – Gespräch über *aluminium extrusion*) und anschließende Diskussion der Ergebnisse
	Grammatikwiederholung	
	Hörverständnis	Ausdrücken von Notwendigkeit und Verpflichtung (Do I have to ...? ... may be needed)
Einsatz von Aluminium, z. B. bei Förderanlagen	Gruppenarbeit	

Technische Hintergrundinformationen

Die folgenden Ausschnitte aus einer Veröffentlichung der Alcoa-Aluminiumwerke zeigen interessante Aspekte der Aluminiumanwendung:

The Ford Motor Company USA is to build a concept car with an extruded aluminium structure. The new Probe V space frame will have only 40 welding points, as compared to 2 000 on Ford's current car frames, and the weight saving offered by aluminium will mean that the car will have a lighter powertrain and suspension than conventional cars, resulting in better fuel economy.

Charles Haddad, manager of advanced engineering for the Ford design staff, said: "The reason we are looking at extruded aluminium is that the investment costs versus that of a stamped steel frame is perhaps ten to one in aluminium's favour." ...

Alform Alloys of Poole, Dorset, and Alcan Wire of Swansea have been working on making aluminium extrusions made by the Conform process more suitable for anodising.
The conform process, which was developed by the UK Atomic Energy Authority, originally used aluminum rod as feed stock, forced through a die to form continuous extrusions. During the process, however, the oxide film on the outside of the rods causes streaks on the extrusion when it is anodised ...

Schlüssel zu den Übungen im Lehrbuch

1. Hörverständnisübung – vergleiche Tapescript im Anhang S. 106
2. a. such   b. half   c. such   d. such   e. half   f. such
3. a. had   b. find   c. arrived   d. have been typing (typed)   e. have known   f. went   g. hasn't finished   h. has been   i. has been   j. have been waiting
4. Hörverständnisübung – vergleiche Tapescript im Anhang S. 107
5. a. got   b. Must   c. must

Anmerkungen und Schlüssel zu den Kopiervorlagen

2. Cost of machine = $5,000.00
   Depreciation at 25% = 1,250.00
   Value at end of first year = 3,750.00
   Depreciation at 10% = 375.00
   Value at end of second year = 3,375.00
   Depreciation at 10% = 337.00
   Value after three years = $3,037.50

3. a. of ... by   b. at   c. on (about)   d. in   e. to   f. at   g. into   h. off
4. a. commenced   b. reducing   c. missed   d. the tools need repairing.   e. You must think of going back ...

Kopiervorlage — Unit 8

1.
Zusätzlicher Text / Diktat:

The latest success story for aluminium in automobiles has been the radiator. The lightweight metal has ousted other materials and taken over 80 % of the European market. Taking advantage of aluminium's lightness, strength, and heat conductivity, the cost-conscious motor industry is concentrating on two methods of making aluminium radiators. One involves mechanical assembly and the industry, clearly aware of the benefits to be gained by reducing weight in as many areas as possible, is investigating and developing many other potential uses of aluminium in rolled, extruded, cast and forged forms.

For many years aluminium has been used in automobile construction where technologies permit the direct substitution of components made from iron-based materials by those made of aluminium alloys. Invariably this has involved castings for engine, gearbox and transmission components.

Such applications are now well established and the scope for aluminium lies in two main directions. First, new concepts are being developed, particularly for the body, that will permit the use of aluminium in conjunction with other modern materials to economically replace steel components. Second, new equipment, designed to improve driving performance, comfort and safety, such as air-conditioning, power-assisted steering and anti-skid-braking systems will benefit from the reduced weight and drag of light-weight aluminium castings.

Aluminium has specific advantages compared with high strength ferrous metals, other light metals, polymers and composite materials. Of these, density, crash behaviour and recycling are particularly important.

What is clear from the development work being carried out is that new designs and techniques are emerging which are overcoming the metal's disadvantages and taking full benefit from its advantages.

2
... and some simple maths:

Your company has bought a new milling machine. The machine, costing $5,000 is estimated to depreciate by 25 % in the first year and by 10 % in each following year. Calculate its value after three years.

Kopiervorlage — Unit 8

3
Fügen Sie eine passende Präposition ein:

a. The use _____ aluminium frames will reduce the cost _____ 10 per cent.

b. They sold the cassette recorder _____ double the price.

c. They phoned us this morning because they wanted to get some information _____ our new model.

d. How long has the new system been _____ operation now?

e. We'll send the drawing _____ their London office.

f. A high DC current is passed _____ a low voltage.

g. The alumina splits _____ aluminium and oxygen.

h. The molten aluminium is siphoned _____ periodically.

4
Schreiben Sie die folgenden Sätze um, ohne dabei den Sinn zu verändern. Ersetzen Sie hierfür die Wörter oder Ausdrücke in Kursivschrift durch die folgenden Verben:

commence / miss / need / reduce / think

a. In our factory volume production *started* in 1993.

_____

b. They're *cutting* our technical staff by a third.

_____

c. We arrived too late at the bus stop, that's why we *didn't catch* the nine o'clock bus this morning.

_____

d. The tools *must be* repaired.

_____

e. You must *remember* to go back to your office this afternoon to meet the new technicians.

_____

9 Working with steel

Lernstoffübersicht – Lehr- und Arbeitsbuch
Schwerpunkte

Themen / Inhalte	Grammatik / Übungen	Situations / Functions
Grundlegende Einführung in die Verwendung und Verarbeitung von Stahl (an Beispielen, besonders Nieten und Schweißen)	Darstellung der Verwendung von Adverbien, hier *fairly, quite, pretty* und *rather* (mit Erläuterungen der Unterschiede und Anwendungsbeispielen)	Erarbeiten eines Textes (mit technischen Zeichnungen und Illustrationen) über die verschiedenen Möglichkeiten, Stahlteile miteinander zu verbinden
Verstehen von relativ einfachen technischen Zeichnungen und Illustrationen	Schriftliche Übung (Zusammmenfassung)	Ratschläge geben / warnen (... *you'd better* ...)

Technische Hintergrundinformationen

<u>fusion welding:</u> any welding operation which involves melting of the base or the parent metal *(= Grundmetall)*.

<u>gas welding:</u> metal welding processes in which gases are used in a combination to obtain a hot flame; the most commonly used gas welding process uses the oxy-acetylene combination which develops a flame temperature of 3,200° C.

<u>laser welding:</u> micro-spot welding *(= Mikroschweißen)* with a laser beam.

<u>metal-arc welding:</u> a type of electric welding in which the electrodes are made of metal and melt during the welding process to form filler metal for the weld.

<u>projection welding:</u> similar to spot welding but allowing a number of welds to be made simultaneously; one of the workpieces has projections at all points or lines to be welded, the other is flat; both are held under pressure between suitable electrodes, and the current flows from one to the other at the contact points of the projections.

<u>resistance seam welding:</u> this process produces a series of individual spot welds, overlapping spot welds, or a continuous nugget weld made by circular or wheel-type electrodes.

<u>spot welding:</u> pieces of sheet are placed together between two electrodes and a heavy current passed while pressure is applied; the result is a nugget of fused metal (somewhat like a rivet) which pins the sheets together.

stud welding: an arc-welding process which uses the heat of an electric arc produced between a metal stud and another part, and then brings the parts together under pressure.

Schlüssel zu den Übungen im Lehrbuch

1. Hörverständnisübung und *note-taking* – vergleiche Tapescript im Anhang S. 107
2. Schriftliche Zusammenfassung des Themas „Aluminium"
3. a. very (quite)   b. quite   c. quite   d. very
4. a. False   b. False   c. True   d. False (first she will ask around)

Anmerkungen und Schlüssel zu den Kopiervorlagen

2. a. linear (alle anderen Begriffe können mit *engineering* kombiniert werden) b. radar (alle anderen Begriffe können mit *welding* kombiniert werden) c. fusion (alle anderen Begriffe können mit *telephone* oder *phone* kombiniert werden)
3. 1. = c / 2. = c / 3. = a / 4. = b / 5. = a / 6. = a / 7. = a / 8. = b / 9. = b / 10. = b / 11. = a
4. a. 16.7ms / b. 2.53s / c. 4.2 years

Kopiervorlage — Unit 9

1
Zusätzlicher Text / Diktat

Galvatite coils and sheets for home trade and for export are delivered in packs to protect the material while in transit and in store. Packs vary according to the customer's requirements and the destination.

Once freely exposed to the air, Galvatite has a life of many years, depending on the environment. However, if moisture is trapped between the laps of a coil or between the sheets in a stack, then the zinc coating can deteriorate quickly, which may lead to water staining (white rust). Therefore, Galvatite should be stored according to the advice given here.

Galvatite should always be stored off the ground, on wooden or metal skids.

It should be stored indoors in a clean, dry area, away from open doorways and sources of chemical pollution. To avoid condensation, which can be caused by rapid changes of temperature, Galvatite should be stored at an even temperature, above the dew point.

If Galvatite has to be stored out of doors, then some simple precautions are essential. If stacks or coils cannot be kept under cover, erect a simple scaffolding around them and cover it with a waterproof sheet, tarpaulin, or polythene. Leave space between the cover and the sheets to allow air to circulate.

Inspect the storage site regularly to ensure that, despite the precautions above, moisture has not penetrated the stack.

white rust = *Weißrost; Zinkrost*
skids = *Kufen*
dew point = *Taupunkt*
scaffolding = *Gerüst*
tarpaulin = *Persenning, geteertes Segeltuch*

2
Welches Wort paßt nicht hinein?
Worauf beziehen sich die Ausdrücke?

a. chemical – civil – electrical – linear – mechanical – process

b. fusion – gas – laser – projection – radar – spot – stud

c. cordless – fusion – pay – portable – cellular – push-button

3
Welche Bedeutung hat *quite* in den folgenden Sätzen:

a. quite = more than "a little" / less than very
b. quite = completely
c. not quite = not completely

1. Well, I'm afraid I didn't quite understand what it was about.
2. We want to leave now. Are you ready? – Not quite.
3. All this sounds quite complicated.
4. I quite agree with you.
5. She wrote a couple of books. She's quite famous.
6. You'd better go inside. It's quite cold.
7. We see each other quite often.
8. Are you sure he repaired the engine? – Yes, I'm quite sure.
9. It's unbelievable. – No, everything they said is quite true.
10. It's quite obvious that something went wrong.
11. He's quite intelligent.

4
... and some simple maths:

Electromagnetic waves travel through the atmosphere at 300,000 km/s, the same speed as through space. How long would a radio signal take to travel ...

a. across the Atlantic Ocean, a distance of 5,000 km?
b. to the Moon and back (Earth to Moon = 380,000 km)?
c. to the nearest star, Proxima Centauri, which is 4.2 light years away?

10 Applying for a job

Lernstoffübersicht – Lehr- und Arbeitsbuch
Schwerpunkte

Themen / Inhalte	Grammatik / Übungen	Situations / Functions
Einführung in Vokabular und Form von Bewerbungsschreiben *(application form / CV / training / letter / envelope)*	Erläuterungen des Gebrauchs von *need* und *needn't* (mit Hinweis auf den Gebrauch von *mustn't*)	Arbeitswelt (Vorstellung eines Bewerbungsformulars einer großen Firma (mit Fragen über Schulung, Ausbildung, Berufserfahrung)
Stellenanzeige (mit entsprechender schriftlicher Aufgabe: Lebenslauf und Bewerbungsschreiben)	Grammatikübungen	Formulierung von Bedingungen, Voraussetzungen und Konsequenzen (... *if* ...)
	Schriftliche Übungen	
	Hörverständnis	

Technische Hintergrundinformationen

site: the position or location of something: They are looking for a site to open a new factory.

Weitere Ausdrücke mit site:
building site = *Baustelle*
on site = *an Ort und Stelle; auf der Baustelle*
on-site facility = *Hilfs- und Nebenanlage auf der Baustelle*
site agent = *Bauleiter*
site equipment = *Baustelleneinrichtung*
site plan = *Lageplan*
well-sited = *schöngelegen*

Schlüssel zu den Übungen im Lehrbuch

1. Gespräch über das Ausfüllen eines Bewerbungsbogens

2. Hörverständnisübung – vergleiche Tapescript im Anhang S. 108

3. a. mustn't   b. mustn't   c. needn't   d. mustn't   e. mustn't   f. needn't

4. A puzzle with numbers:

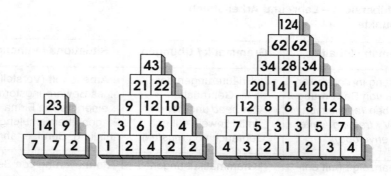

5. Erstellen eines Lebenslaufs und eines Bewerbungsschreibens
6. a. would   b. had ... would   c. would   d. had had ... would   e. would   f. Would
   g. would
7. a. True   b. False   c. True   d. False   e. False   f. False
8. a. any   b. Some   c. some   d. some
9. a. No, you needn't write all the reports now, you can write them (on) Monday or Tuesday. b. No, she needn't speak with the chief engineer today, she can speak with him tomorrow afternoon. c. No, we (you) needn't test the brakes this morning, we (you) can test them when we (you) are at the garage tomorrow. d. No, we needn't check the milling machine right away, we can check it later. e. No, we needn't replace the chip before they start work, we can replace it afterwards.

Anmerkungen und Schlüssel zu den Kopiervorlagen

2. Beispiele: If I had a computer ... I'd be able to work more accurately / ... I'd be able to save time / ... I could make better drawings / ... I could work at home.
3. a. needn't   b. mustn't   c. must   d. needn't   e. must   f. mustn't
4. a. 1hr 15mins / b. 10
5. Rollenspiel: Telefongespräch
6. schriftliches Erstellen eines Bewerbungsschreibens und eines Lebenslaufs
7. Muster eines Lebenslaufs

| Kopiervorlage | Unit 10 |

1
Zusätzlicher Text / Diktat

Der folgende Text aus einem kanadischen Prospekt beschreibt die Ziele eines Lehrgangs zur Ausbildung auf dem Gebiet von *Power and Process Engineering* (= Energie- und Verfahrenstechnik)

Graduates of this program will have acquired the skills and knowledge to:

- demonstrate an understanding of the principles of engineering mechanics and thermal engineering to a level comparable to second year university;
- accept and perform the duties of a Third Class Power Engineer in an industrial power plant;
- understand thoroughly the chemistry, metallurgy, theories of fuels and combustion, and maintenance and control of equipment necessary for the safe operation of a large industrial power plant;
- operate and maintain the instruments and control systems associated with large steam plants;
- operate electrical equipment such as Direct Current (DC) machinery, Alternating Current (AC) motors and generators, transformers, circuit breakers, and associated safety devices;
- make drawings of mechanical and electrical equipment according to accepted drafting standards;
- apply the principles and techniques of industrial organization and communication;
- give and receive oral instructions and give demonstrations;
- demonstrate a thorough familiarity with boiler construction details and operation;
- operate and maintain all power plant auxiliary equiment.

Kopiervorlage Unit 10

2
Gruppenarbeit

Jede Gruppe versucht, die leeren Felder mit einem passenden Satzteil zu füllen, so daß jeweils ein sinnvoller Satz entsteht. Anschließend vergleichen die Gruppen ihre Sätze.

Beispiel: *If I had a computer I'd be able to work much faster.*

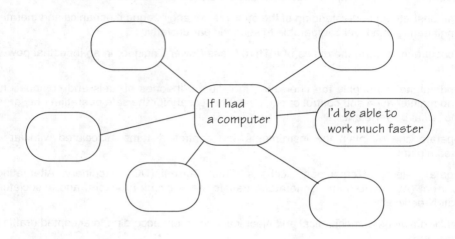

3
Setzen Sie *must*, *mustn't* oder *needn't* in die Lücken ein:

a. Our modem is fast enough for our kind of work. We _____ buy a faster one.

b. We need the spare parts urgently. We _____ forget to order them first thing tomorrow morning.

c. We haven't got much time left. We _____ finish our job as quickly as possible.

d. They want to speak to you personally. You _____ send them a report.

e. I don't speak any Spanish at all but if I want this job I _____ learn the language rather quickly.

f. You _____ use this plug. It's damaged.

Kopiervorlage   Unit 10

4
... and some maths:

a. An electric water pump is able to pump water at a rate of 12 gallons per minute. How long would it take to fill a 900 gallon tank?

b. If a lathe rotates at 600rpm, how many times does it rotate in one second?

5
Rollenspiel für 3 Kursteilnehmer/innen – Telephone Conversation

Ein Kursteilnehmer/eine Kursteilnehmerin möchte sich um die auf der nächsten Seite abgebildete Stelle bewerben und ruft Witter Engineering Services PLC an, um sich mit der Personalabteilung verbinden zu lassen. Die Zentrale (ein anderer Kursteilnehmer) nimmt das Gespräch an und stellt durch. Jemand aus der Personalabteilung (eine weitere Kursteilnehmerin) nimmt das Gespräch entgegen. Es geht hauptsächlich um einen Termin für ein persönliches Vorstellungsgespräch.

Kopiervorlage   **Unit 10**

6
Schriftliche Übung

Sie setzen ein Bewerbungsschreiben und einen Lebenslauf für die ausgeschriebene Stelle auf.

WITTER

DESIGN ENGINEERS

Witter Engineering provide a comprehensive design, project management and construction service for heavy process plant and equipment, specialising in turnkey continuous casting plants for the steel industry.

We are seeking well qualified ambitious Design Engineers to work on a variety of challenging new projects, at a number of levels of responsibility.

You will have a University Degree, with a successful background in heavy process plant design, including heavy fabrication associated with close tolerance machining or the selection of water plant, hydraulic systems and general services pipework.

Based at our offices at Workington, the positions will involve occasional visits to clients, suppliers and to our construction sites.

Excellent negotiable starting salaries, large company benefits and relocation assistance where appropriate will accompany good prospects for career development within a progressive and rapidly developing company.

Please send a full cv or write or telephone for an application form to:

WITTER ENGINEERING SERVICES PLC
P.O. Box 2, Workington, Cumbria CA142JJ
Tel: Workington (0900) / 04389

7

Resumé*

NAME:	Bruce Thomson
HOME ADDRESS:	876 Woodbridge Road West, Columbus, Ohio Telephone (612) 445–0739
DATE OF BIRTH:	October 12, 1967
PLACE OF BIRTH:	Austin, Texas
MARITAL STATUS:	Single
EDUCATION:	Lavitt High School, Columbus, Ohio Graduated 1986 Alantown University, Madison, Wisconsin 1986–1990 B. S. in Computer Science Norris University College, New York, New York 1990–1992 Industrial Engineering and Operations Research
PROFESSIONAL EXPERIENCE:	Curtiss Motor Design Corporation, Alison, New Jersey Trainee program: Systems Development January 1993–January 1994 Albington Aluminum Inc., St. Paul, Minnesota Systems Analyst February 1994–February 1995
CURRENT POSITION:	Carney Instruments Inc., Columbus, Ohio Sales Engineer for electronic components March 1995–present
FOREIGN LANGUAGES:	Spanish
INTERESTS:	Football; Spanish literature; History of Mexico
REFERENCES:	Provided on request

* American English: Resumé
British English: Curriculum vitae (CV)

Testing Your Language   Part One

A. Reading comprehension
   1 = c
   2 = d
   3 = a und d
   4 = a

B. Listening comprehension
   1. a = True; b = False
   2. a = True; b. = False
   3. a = False; b = True
   4. a = False; b = True

C. Listening comprehension
   1. = b
   2. = c
   3. = c
   4. = c

11 Testing and finishing (1)

Lernstoffübersicht – Lehr- und Arbeitsbuch
Schwerpunkte

Themen / Inhalte	Grammatik / Übungen	Situations / Functions
Einführung in den Bereich Design und Endbearbeitung (z.B. Galvanisieren und Beschichten von Werkstoffen) / Voraussetzungen für haltbare Bearbeitung (z. B. Formgebung und Materialwahl Konstruktion	*Present Perfect / Past Perfect*, hier besonders in der Verlaufsform Diskussions- und Sprechübung (auf der Basis von Bildvorlagen) Textverstehen (Text über Metallbearbeitung)	Arbeitsleben (hier: auf dem Weg zur Fabrik) Etwas klassifizieren / beschreiben / Orte angeben (z. B. *Which box do these transistors go into? / All the ladders stood against the wall.*)

Technische Hintergrundinformationen

Für die Mehrzahlbildung technisch-wissenschaftlicher Wörter gibt es verschiedene Möglichkeiten (erste Mehrzahlangabe = *"English Plural"*, zweite Mehrzahlangabe = *"Foreign Plural"*):

album / albums / —
analysis / —/ analyses [əˈnæləsiːz]
antenna / antennas / antennae [ænˈteniː]
apparatus / apparatuses / —
appendix / appendixes / appendices [əˈpendɪsiːz]
axis / —/ axes [ˈæksiːz]
cactus / cactuses / cacti [ˈkæktaɪ]
crisis / —/ crises [ˈkraɪsiːz]
criterion / —/ criteria
formula / formulas / formulae [ˈfɔːmjʊliː]
genius / geniuses / —
index / indexes / indices [ˈɪndɪsiːz]
medium / mediums / media
parenthesis [pəˈrenθɪsɪs] / —/ parentheses [pəˈrenθɪsiːz]
phenomenon / phenomenons / phenomena
radius / —/ radii [ˈreɪdɪaɪ]
schema /schemas / schemata [ˈskiːmətə]
stratum / —/ strata
tempo / tempos / tempi [ˈtempiː]
trapezium / trapeziums / trapezia [trəˈpiːzjə]

Anmerkung: antennas = on a radio; antennae = on an insect
press, TV, etc. = only media

Schlüssel zu den Übungen im Lehrbuch

1. Mögliche Antworten:
   Fins = not OK; Rolling edges = OK; Hollow articles (drain holes) = OK; Corners and edges = OK; Slots = not OK; Bends = OK; Blind holes = OK; Ribs = OK (not mentioned in text)

2. a. gave   b. stood / were standing   c. been using   d. had already gone (away)
   e. had been working   f. been trying

3. Hörverständnisübung und *note-taking* – vergleiche Tapescript im Anhang S. 111

4. a. Because they had been working all day.   b. ... learning ...   c. ... writing ...
   d. ... washing ...   e. ... repairing ...   f. .... talking ...   g. ... making ...   h. ... talking ...
   i. .... programming ...

5. Bildgesteuertes Gespräch über Gefahren im Alltag

Anmerkungen und Schlüssel zu den Kopiervorlagen

2. Offene Kommunikationsübung

3. a. at ... of   b. in   c. with   d. into (in)   e. to   f. with   g. of ... off   h. for   i. out

4. Beispiele in der Reihenfolge der A-Gruppe:
   corrosion resistance / curriculum vitae / electrical appliance / fork lift truck / frequency ranges / garment storage / laser printer / metal finishing / tape speed / training facilities / voltage conversion

Kopiervorlage — Unit 11

1
Zusätzlicher Text / Diktat

One approach to protecting metallic components against corrosion is to coat them with a suitable polymeric material. Plastic Coatings of Guildford offers some 40 different coatings of this type based on fluoroplastic compounds with various other additives. They incorporate such well-tried materials as Teflon and Fluoroplas. Such coatings will resist the *ASTM B-117* 3000-hours salt spray test and have been successfully applied to fasteners used in the offshore industry, where corrosion from sea water is a major problem and where such a coating provides the means of undoing an otherwise seized bolt. Fasteners, clips and small components coated with these materials also withstand the salt-spray tests demanded by the motor industry. Fluorocarbon-coated carburettor and brake components, with dry lubricant properties, result in more efficient mechanical operation as well as resistance to attack from petroleum/methanol mixtures.
Chemical resistance in the process industries is provided by high-performance specialist dispersion finishes, many of which can be used at temperatures up to 200°C.

2
Erzählen Sie etwas über sich und benutzen Sie dabei, je nachdem, entweder *Present Perfect* oder *Past Tense*. Berücksichtigen Sie dabei die folgenden Punkte:

a. move here in / live here for ...

b. serve an apprenticeship / study

c. start work at present company ...

d. work in present job ...

e. never be to ...

f. never seen ...

g. have a car / bicycle / motorbike since (for) ...

h. marry in ... / never marry

i. read a technical journal / magazine / newspaper regularly since (for) ...

j. learn technical English since (for) ...

k. start learn technical English ...

l. attend this course / start this course ...

Kopiervorlage   Unit 11

3
Fügen Sie eine passende Präposition ein:

a. When you look _____ the illustration, you will see that corners should have radii _____ _____ least 1mm.

b. This material has a very good corrosion resistance _____ most environments.

c. Fasteners coated _____ these substances withstand most salt-spray tests.

d. As far as I know, this module goes _____ this slot her.

e. If I were you, I would not invite him _____ the party.

f. We should not wait too long _____ our renovation programme.

g. Because _____ a snowstorm, the plane took _____ over an hour late.

h. He does not know what the initials "CAD" stand _____.

i. It is easy to make a plan, but it is much harder to carry it _____.

4
Verbinden Sie einen Ausdruck aus der Gruppe A mit einem passenden Ausdruck aus der Gruppe B:

A	B
corrosion	appliances
curriculum	conversion
electrical	facilities
fork lift	finishing
frequency	printer
garment	ranges
laser	resistance
metal	speed
tape	storage
training	truck
voltage	vitae

12 Testing and finishing (2)

voltage   vitae

Themen / Inhalte	Grammatik / Übungen	Situations / Functions
Zweiter Teil der Einführung in den Bereich Testen und Endbearbeitung (hier: Vorstellung eines Rohrofens für die Analyse)	Grundlegende Einführung in den Grammatikbereich	Schreiben eines Briefes an eine Beratungsstelle für Camcorder-Probleme
	„Indirekte Rede" Textverstehen (Darstellung eines Rohrofens)	Etwas klassifizieren / beschreiben / Orte angeben (z. B. ... should be mounted on the roof / ... is located at the bottom)
Vorstellung eines kurzen Briefes (mit entsprechender Aufgabenstellung)	Hörverständnis	
	Wortschatzübung	

Lernstoffübersicht – Lehr- und Arbeitsbuch
Schwerpunkte

Technische Hintergrundinformation

<u>calibrate:</u> check, adjust, or systematically standardize the graduations of a quantitative measuring instrument *(= kalibrieren)*.

<u>thermocouple:</u> a device which consists of two different conductors joined together at their ends; the thermoelectric voltage developed between the two junctions is proportional to the temperature difference between the junctions; thermocouples can be used to measure the temperature of one of the junctions when the other is held at a fixed, known temperature, or to convert radiant energy into electric energy *(= Thermoelement)*.

Schlüssel zu den Übungen im Lehrbuch

1. Fragen zum Text *Tube Furnaces*
2. Hörverständnisübung – vergleiche Tapescript im Anhang S. 111

Anmerkungen und Schlüssel zu den Kopiervorlagen

2. Beispiele:
   ... that he was going to drive ... / ... that he had tested ... / ... that I had forgotten ... / ... that our company was bankrupt ... / .... that they had had some engine trouble ... / ... that they had to find ...
3. accelerator = 5 / battery = 1 / catalyst = 8 / expansion = 3 / switch = 6 / thermometer = 4 / triangle = 2 / velocity = 7
4. It is the flight attendants always running back and forth who travel the greatest distance!

| Kopiervorlage | Unit 12 |

1
Zusätzlicher Text / Diktat:

1.0 OPERATING INSTRUCTIONS

1.1 Switch on the electrical supply. The red "mains" light should glow.

1.2 Operate the instrument switch, located close to the "mains" light, to activate the temperature controller. One or more lights on the controller will become illuminated.

1.3 Close the door and adjust the temperature controller.

1.4 The furnace will now begin to heat up. The orange heater light will glow steadily at first and then flash as the furnace approaches the desired temperature.

1.5 Operating Temperature. Heating element life is shortened by use at temperatures close to maximum. Do not leave the furnace at high temperature when not required. If in doubt, the maximum temperature is shown on the specification plate.

1.6 Do not put towels etc. over the furnace cooling vents. They must remain unobstructed to keep the electrical controls cool.

1.7 Loading and Unloading. Avoid burns. Carbolite can supply tongs, face masks, and heat resistant gloves. Before you remove a hot object from the furnace make sure you have a safe place to put it down.

When heating large objects (in particular poor conductors) take care to avoid shielding the thermocouple from the heating elements.

The thermocouple normally senses the heating element temperature. If a large cold object is placed in the chamber the thermocouple may record the average of the object and the element temperatures. This can lead to overheating of the elements. Allow the object to gain heat at a lower temperature before setting the furnace to a temperature close to the maximum.

1.8 Door Switch – All chamber furnaces (except those with mineral insulated elements) incorporate a safety switch which interrupts the heating element circuit when the door is opened. This prevents the user touching a live heating element – but, of course, the furnace will not heat up if the door is left open.

1.9 Ventilation – If the furnace is to be used for heating materials which produce smoke or fumes, the chimney must be correctly fitted and unobstructed. Otherwise, soot will accumulate in the chamber and between the layers of insulation, causing an electrical breakdown of the heating elements. Furnaces used for this kind of application must be heated regularly up to maximum temperature and held for one hour to burn away the soot.

Kopiervorlage — Unit 12

2
Berichten Sie, was Mr Miller Ihnen gesagt hat. Zum Beispiel:

He told me that ...
He said that ...

> I'm going to drive to London on Monday /
> I tested the materials last week /
> You have forgotten to order the replacement tools /
> Our company is bankrupt, I'm afraid /
> We had some engine trouble yesterday /
> We must find a more cost effective solution

3
Welche Erklärung paßt zu welchem Wort?

a. accelerator
b. battery
c. catalyst
d. expansion
e. switch
f. thermometer
g. triangle
h. velocity

1. device that produces electricity e.g. in a radio
2. figure (three-sided) with three angles
3. increase in volume caused by heat
4. instrument used for measuring the temperature of a room
5. pedal in a vehicle which increases its speed
6. something which opens or closes an electric circuit
7. speed at which something moves in a given direction
8. substance that increases the rate of a chemical reaction

4
... just for fun:

A plane is going to leave Frankfurt for Dallas. It is fully booked, and the passengers and crew are all ready. Can you work out which person will have travelled the greatest distance by the time the plane arrives in Dallas?

13 Plastics in daily use

Lernstoffübersicht – Lehr- und Arbeitsbuch
Schwerpunkte

Themen / Inhalte	Grammatik / Übungen	Situations / Functions
Kurze Einführung in den Bereich Kunststoffe und deren Verwendung sowie Kunststoffrecycling	Ausdrücke mit *take*, wie z. B. *take the blame, How long will it take?*	Hören / Verstehen eines Textes über Kunststoffe und Abfallprobleme
Vervollständigen eines teilweise vorgegebenen Textes (auf der Basis einer Hörverständnisübung)	Grammatikübung (mit *get, go* und *take*)	Ausdrücke und Formulierungen mit Zeitangaben (z. B. *When's your appointment? / ... when you've finished greasing / ... within ...*)
	Hörverständnis	
	Diskussion (Recycling)	

Technische Hintergrundinformationen

<u>incinerator:</u> a furnace for burning trash or garbage *(= Abfallverbrennungsofen, Müllverbrennungsanlage)*

<u>landfill</u> (mainly US): a system of trash and garbage disposal in which the waste is buried between layers of earth to build up low-lying land *(= Mülldeponie)*.

<u>resin:</u> any of several yellowish or brownish sticky substances that ooze from pine, balsam, and certain other trees and plants; resin is used in making varnishes, lacquers, plastics, and many other products *(= Harz)*.

Schlüssel zu den Übungen im Lehrbuch

1. a. 900 pounds   b. 40,000   c. 15%   d. 10%   e. Millions
2. a. go   b. go   c. take   d. get   e. get   f. get   g. get   h. get   i. go   j. get   k. get   l. take   m. get   n. go
3. Hörverständnisübung – vergleiche Tapescript im Anhang S. 113

Anmerkungen und Schlüssel zu den Kopiervorlagen

2. Fragen zum Text im Coursebook Seite 79
3.

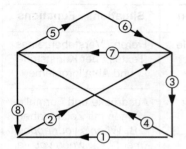

4. Beispiele:
   sailboards / printed circuits / carpets / containers / machine parts / clothes / car components
5. Offene Kommunikationsübung

| Kopiervorlage | Unit 13 |

1
Zusätzlicher Text / Diktat

Spills and drips from coffee, wine and food can stain the brilliant beauty of furniture fabric ... especially in restaurants, offices and lounges. But those annoying splashes and drips aren't going to cast their ugly shadow on furniture much longer because Amoco Fabrics and Fibers has developed a brilliant new fiber that repels moisture and stains, so furniture colors stay true for years.
Known as Trace™, the new yarn provides international furniture manufacturers with durability and strength, making it ideal for use with contract furniture. Trace yarn's wearability comes, in part, from its polypropylene base. A unique chemical with exceptional resistance to moisture and humidity, polypropylene enables Trace to repel food and beverage drips, spills, and drops – without a sign of any leftovers.
Moisture resistance enables Trace yarns to fare well in high-humidity areas, such as atriums, cafeterias and spas, too. The fibers absorb an insignificant amount of moisture when exposed to dampness and wetness.
According to Georgia-based Amoco fabrics and fibers, a special solution-dying process is used to lock color tightly into each thread, for an exceptionally intense and lasting hue. So even in a corporate solarium, where sunshine beats down, Trace remains vivid and bright.
Colorful, durable and lasting, this new yarn is helping manufacturers worldwide create more attractive corporate and office furniture that's turning everyday business into an uncommon pleasure.

2
Coursebook page 79: Questions on the text.

a. What does the text say about "growth" in the chemical industry?

b. What kind of people work at Amoco?

c. What kind of specialized research facilities do they have and why?

d. What is the purpose of the recycling project in New York?

e. Why are the foam packing crates useful for fruits and vegetables?

f. What are the special characteristics of hybrid resins and the carpets?

g. What is "Scotchgard"?

Kopiervorlage — Unit 13

3
... a brain teaser

Have a look at the envelope on the right. Can you draw such an envelope without taking your pencil of the page and without going over any line twice? (In other words, you have to do it in a single, unbroken line.)

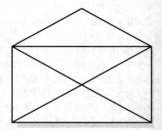

4
Wortfelder (Gruppenarbeit)

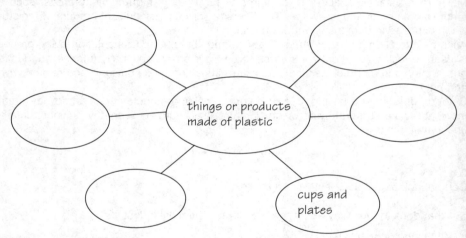

Jede Gruppe versucht, die leeren Felder mit einem passenden Begriff aus dem Wortfeldbereich zu füllen.
Anschließend vergleichen die einzelnen Gruppen ihre Ergebnisse.

5
Group discussion – Schauen Sie sich die Ergebnisse in den Wortfeldern noch einmal an und diskutieren Sie die folgenden Fragen:

1. How can the plastic things or products above be recycled?

2. Why is it important to recycle them?

14 The Docklands Light Railway

Lernstoffübersicht – Lehr- und Arbeitsbuch
Schwerpunkte

Themen / Inhalte	Grammatik / Übungen	Situations / Functions
Stadtbahnsysteme, hier besonders Stadtbahnen auf eigenem Gleiskörper *(light rail)* mit den entsprechenden Steuer- und Überwachungsanlagen (Computersteuerung)	Vollendete Gegenwart *(simple past perfect)*, mit Hinweis auf die Unterschiede zu *Simple Past*	Verstehen von Text und Photos in Verbindung mit Hörverständnis
	Ausfüllen eines Berichtsformulars	Wünsche formulieren / ausdrücken (z. B. *We'd like to copy ... / We'd greatly appreciate your comments / We only wish we could ...*)
Erstellen eines Unfallberichts	Präpositionen	

Technische Hintergrundinformationen

light rail transit: also known as light rapid transit, it is a form of transportation that fits between the spheres of bus and conventional heavy railway operation; there are, it is estimated, over 300 systems in operation around the world; the Docklands system combines automatic operation with the retention of staff on trains, having a sophisticated signalling and control system but no lineside signals; with relatively small vehicles and the consequent possibility of tighter track curves, such systems can often weave around existing townscapes, avoiding the need for extensive urban disruption; they do not need similar levels of staffing to heavy rail, yet at the same time they can cope admirably with passengers flows far in excess of those catered for by buses; compared with buses, light rail can be fast, quiet and smooth.

Schlüssel zu den Übungen im Lehrbuch

1. Offene Kommunikationsübung zum Thema *Automatic train operation and protection system (ATO/ATP)*

2.

DOCKLANDS LIGHT RAILWAY

**PRELIMINARY
ACCIDENT REPORT**

NAME: _Millikan_

FIRST NAME: _Roy_

DATE OF ACCIDENT: _(today)_

TIME OF ACCIDENT: _10:30_

PLACE OF ACCIDENT: _car park outside OMC_

POSITION IN COMPANY: _train driver_

TYPE OF INJURY: _two fingers broken (slipped)_

IN HOSPITAL? _no_

IF YES, WHERE? _____

---

3. Hörverständnisübung – vergleiche Tapescript im Anhang S. 114
4. a. of   b. above   c. in   d. to   e. by   f. out

Anmerkungen und Schlüssel zu den Kopiervorlagen

2. a. of ... by   b. at ... in (from)   c. by (with) ... in ... on ... under ... at   d. up   e. in (under) ... of ... to
3. a. The train had already left when I arrived ...   b. The meeting had already been cancelled at short notice when I arrived.   c. The cheaper models had already been sold when I arrived at the shop.   d. The new American manual had already been translated into German.
4. a. always   b. yet   c. yet   d. always   e. yet (= schon wieder)

Kopiervorlage — Unit 14

1
Zusätzlicher Text / Diktat

Control systems ensure the safety of people, the reliability of industrial processes and the protection of the environment. They act as the interface between man and the industrial process being monitored. Their tasks include not only the control and monitoring of the process but also such items as optimisation, situation analysis, invoicing etc. High availability and visibility of the process for the personnel must be ensured. The fulfilment of these requirements has only become possible due to the rapid development of microelectronics. High computing speeds, large memory capacity, short access times and the use of modular software make it possible to execute complex process tasks. For display purposes, colour graphic systems have become very important. In addition to the display of data on screens, modern control systems also permit interactive user operating functions.
This development is drastically changing conventional control consoles and control rooms. The industrial process is displayed on colour TV screens in the form of schematic diagrams of the plant, flow diagrams, curve displays and texts, using freely definable symbols. The screen indicates current events by showing data for all the parameters concerned, including pressures, temperatures, oil levels, flow rates and weights. This type of priority-oriented display makes it easier for the operator to correlate measurement data to measurement points. Curve displays illustrate the trends in the process clearly, so that the approaching of limits can be recognised at a glance. Interactive guidance of the operator is effected by means of text displays in the form of menus.

2
Fügen Sie eine passende Präposition ein:

a. The movement _____ the train is monitored _____ a conventional signalling system.

b. The boat service will start _____ Chelsea Harbour _____ September.

c. The system is operated _____ eleven vehicles – nine are _____ service and two are _____ standby or _____ maintenance _____ any time.

d. Each vehicle has standing room for _____ to 140 passengers.

e. The vehicles are fully automatic and, _____ normal conditions, the only responsibility _____ the operator is _____ close the doors.

Kopiervorlage — Unit 14

3
Was war inzwischen geschehen? Bilden Sie Sätze mit *had:*

a. You went to the station to catch the eight o'clock train to London. When you arrived at the station the train was no longer there. (train / leave already)

_____

_____

b. You went to a business meeting. When you arrived there you didn't see any of your colleagues. (meeting / cancel at short notice)

_____

_____

c. Your local shop offered computers at reduced prices. When you went there to buy one you didn't see any. (cheaper models / sell already)

_____

_____

d. You received a new American technical manual. When you wanted to translate it into German your colleagues told you that this was not necessary. (manual / translate into German already)

_____

_____

4
Always oder *yet*?

a. I have _____ wanted to travel to Alaska during the summer.

b. Have you had your lunch _____?

c. It will not be dark for half an hour _____.

d. That soft drink machine is terrible – it's _____ out of order!

e. I am sorry to bring up this subject _____ again.

15 Cleaning the air

Lernstoffübersicht – Lehr- und Arbeitsbuch
Schwerpunkte

Themen / Inhalte	Grammatik / Übungen	Situations / Functions
Einführung in die Konstruktion und Verwendung von Klimaanlagen in Fahrzeugen und Fabriken (mit dem entsprechenden Wortschatz und Zeichnungen)	Kurze Einführung in den Grammatikbereich „Konditionalsätze"	Verstehen einer technischen Zeichnung / Planung einer Fahrt nach London zum Science Museum
	Textverstehen (Originaltext aus einer amerikanischen Firmenbroschüre)	Ausdrücken des Sachverhalts „es spielt keine Rolle", „es ist schon in Ordnung"
Darstellung verschiedener *skills* mit Diskussion	Hörverständnis und *Note-taking*	

Technische Hintergrundinformationen

<u>hi-fi</u> ['haɪ'faɪ] (= high fidelity ['haɪfɪ'delətɪ]): an electronic system for reproducing high-fidelity sound from radio, records, CDs, or magnetic tape.

<u>spark plug:</u> GB also: <u>sparking plug</u> *(Zündkerze)*

<u>tile:</u> a thin slab or piece of baked clay, plastic, porcelain, or other material; tiles are laid in rows and used to cover floors, walls, or roofs.

<u>tune</u> (also: <u>tune up</u>): to adjust an engine to efficient working order *(= einstellen, abstimmen) (Der deutsche Ausdruck Tuning = Frisieren wird im Englischen mit* tuning for performance *wiedergegeben – er darf also nicht mit dem englischen* tune *oder* tune up *verwechselt werden.)*

Schlüssel zu den Übungen im Lehrbuch

1. Hörverständnisübung und *note-taking* – vergleiche Tapescript im Anhang S. 115
2. Gespräch über *Are you handy with tools?*
3. Hörverständnisübung und *note-taking* – vergleiche Tapescript im Anhang S. 115
4. a. = 2 / b. = 2 / c. = 2 / d. = 3 / e. = 2 / f. = 3 / g. = 3
5. a. When   b. yet   c. if   d. now   e. If
6. Beschreibung eines technischen Vorgangs

Anmerkungen und Schlüssel zu den Kopiervorlagen

2. Beispiele in der Reihenfolge der A-Gruppe:
   If you are not yet one of our customers, give us a chance. / If you had more cash at your disposal, you would certainly be able to build a terminal that could handle a lot more passengers. / If you had seen our latest sales figures, you would have worried more. / If you had taken the earlier train, you would have arrived in time. / If your systems are not too expensive, companies will buy them.

3. a. Industrial southeast ... more than twenty years b. conditioning ... filtration c. hi-tech clean rooms ... textile production areas, process piping, and metal fabrication d. Greensboro, North Carolina e. the need exists

4. a. had   b. would   c. would   d. Would   e. had   f. would

5. The man reaches the island by placing his two planks as shown below in one of the corners. One plank is placed diagonally aross the corner and the second at right angles to the first.

| Kopiervorlage | Unit 15 |

1
Zusätzlicher Text / Diktat

Air conditioning works very much like a refrigerator. It is based on two principles:
1. When any liquid becomes a vapour or gas, it absorbs heat, and conversely, when a vapour becomes a liquid, it gives off heat;
2. heat always moves from a warmer spot to a cooler spot. Air conditioning does not add cold, it removes heat from one area and sends it to another area through the use of a fluid called refrigerant.

All air conditioning components – compressor, evaporator, condenser, blower motor, receiver and expansion valve – must be in good working order. The best thing you can do to keep your air conditioning in healthy working order is to run the system once a week whenever the outside temperature is above 50 degrees F. The many rubber seals that join different components of this system will dry and crack if not lubricated by the oil that is added to the system and that circulates with the refrigerant. It only lubricates when the air conditioning is on.

evaporator = *Verdampfer*
receiver = *Zwischenbehälter*
expansion valve = *Drosselventil*

2
Bilden Sie sinnvolle Sätze, indem Sie jeweils einen Teil von A und einen Teil von B nehmen:

A	B
If you are not yet one of our customers ...	companies will buy them.
If you had more cash at your disposal ...	give us a chance.
If you had seen our latest sales figures ...	you would have arrived in time.
If you had taken the earlier train ...	you would have worried more.
If your systems are not too expensive ...	you would certainly be able to build a terminal that could handle a lot more passengers.

Kopiervorlage — Unit 15

3

Schauen Sie sich den Text **Air Conditioning: For New and Existing Systems** noch einmal an und vervollständigen Sie die Sätze:

a. Industrial Air, Inc. has served the _____ for _____ .

b. The areas they now serve are: air _____ and _____ .

c. The applications range from _____ to _____ .

d. Their facilities are located in _____ .

e. Their representatives will travel to your location when _____ .

4
Had oder *would*?

a. When the letter of complaint arrived, we _____ already dispatched the components by airmail.

b. They sent us a letter saying that they _____ appreciate our help.

c. What I _____ like to know is where the accident happened.

d. _____ you like to know the price of the raw materials?

e. I wish we _____ been able to meet their deadline!

f. I wish he _____ not call me every morning.

5
... and a brain teaser:

A man wants to get to the island shown on the right. This island is surrounded by a moat of regular width, but very deep and impossible to jump across. The man has two planks, exactly as long as the moat is wide. Therefore, he cannot place the planks across the moat. How then can he get across to the island without getting wet?

16 Working with a machining center

Lernstoffübersicht – Lehr- und Arbeitsbuch
Schwerpunkte

Themen / Inhalte	Grammatik / Übungen	Situations / Functions
Vorstellung eines Bearbeitungszentrums mit verschiedenen Funktionen – *machining center*, mit dem entsprechenden Wortschatz und Schnittzeichnungen	Vorstellung von *as, because* und *since* und Darstellung in Beispielsätzen (in der Bedeutung von „weil", „da")	Gespräche mit Arbeitskollegen und -kolleginnen
		Verstehen von Beschreibungen und Zeichnungen
	Hörverständnis	Ausdruck von Zustimmung und Kritik (*... very satisfactory / ... not really adequate ...*)
Eintragung von Daten in eine Tabelle	Leseverstehen (mit Fragen zumText)	

Technische Hintergrundinformationen

<u>CNC</u> (= computer numerical control): a system in which numerical values corresponding to desired tool or control positions are generated by a computer.

<u>machining center:</u> manufacturing equipment that removes metal under computer numerical control by making use of several axes and a variety of tools and operations.

Weitere gebräuchliche Ausdrücke auf der Basis von <u>machine</u>:
<u>to machine</u> = *maschinell bearbeiten*
<u>machine attendant</u> = *Maschinenwärter, Maschinist*
<u>machine downtime</u> = *Maschinenausfallzeit*
<u>machine fitter</u> = *Monteur, Maschinenschlosser*
<u>machine hour</u> = *Maschinenstunde*
<u>machine tool</u> = *Werkzeugmaschine*
<u>machinery</u> = *1. Maschinerie, Triebwerk; 2. Maschinenpark*
<u>machinable</u> = *maschinell bearbeitbar*
<u>machinability</u> = *maschinelle Bearbeitbarkeit*

<u>sophisticated:</u> 1) formed by or showing worldly experience, cultivation, education, etc.: a sophisticated taste in food; a sophisticated audience *(= intellektuell; geistig anspruchsvoll)*; 2) artificial, not natural or simple: Their conversation was only sophisticated chatter *(= blasiert, pseudo-intellektuell, „hochgestochen")*; 3) highly complicated or developed; complex: sophisticated control equipment *(= hochentwickelt, technisch ausgereift)*.

Schlüssel zu den Übungen im Lehrbuch

1.

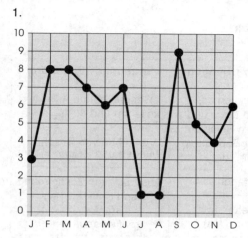

2. Die beiden Linien sind gleich lang!
3. a. because   b. because   c. although   d. because
4. Fragen zum Text und einer technischen Zeichnung
5. Hörverständnisübung – vergleiche Tapescript im Anhang S. 116
6. a. really   b. really   c. very   d. really   e. really   f. really   g. really   h. very   i. really
7. Summe der linken Spalte: 16; Zahlenwerte:

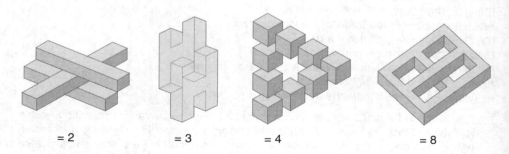

Anmerkungen und Schlüssel zu den Kopiervorlagen

2. und 3. sind offene Kommunikationsübungen.

| Kopiervorlage | Unit 16 |

1
Zusätzlicher Text / Diktat:

KT-Swasey, Milwaukee, provides two types of machine improvements, both of which will result in a better, more productive, more reliable machine:

Remanufacturing. The entire machine is systematically dismantled down to the bare casting, and every part is steam-cleaned and inspected. All bearings, seals, and other common high-wear parts are replaced, regardless of condition. The ways are either re-ground or replaced.

The machine is then carefully reassembled. A new control – the same control that goes into a new machine – is installed. After final assembly, the machine is inspected, aligned and calibrated. A standard cutting is also run to ensure the machine alignments and accuracies under actual cutting conditions. A 48-hour shakedown is run to ensure machine reliability before the machine is painted and returned in like-new condition. The complete machine carries a one-year warranty – the same warranty that covers a new machine.

Control Retrofitting. The machine is thoroughly inspected by a KT-Swasey serviceman to ensure its reliability prior to control retrofit. If any mechanical repairs are necessary, parts can be ordered so the repairs can be done during the retrofit program.

New control features, not available when your machine was built, simplify programming, machine operation and maintenance while increasing the productivity of your machine. These new features can often accommodate mechanical updates such as tool gaging, multiple pallet storage and cell integration to increase part accuracy and reduce the demands of operator intervention and attention.

And when retrofitting – like remanufacturing – is complete, your machine and its added capabilities carry a one-year warranty on the retrofitted control and its associated components.

It's all part of KT-Swasey's commitment to the customer. Tell us what your manufacturing requirements are, and our Renewment Operations team will help you meet those requirements. If you want to add a machine or replace an existing machine with a remanufactured one, we'll help you find a used model that meets your needs, and we'll perform the remanufacture on it. And if you have a machine or machines that you want renewed, we can stagger the remanufacturing process so that your downtime is reduced, your productivity is maintained and your manufacturing process is disrupted as little as possible.

<u>remanufacturing</u> = *Grundüberholung*
<u>cutting conditions</u> = *Schnittgröße*
<u>shakedown</u> = *Versuchslauf*
<u>retrofitting</u> = *Nachrüstung*
<u>tool gaging (GB: gauging)</u> = *Werkzeugeichung*

Kopiervorlage	Unit 16

2

Machen Sie sich Notizen über die wesentlichen Punkte der Sicherheitsanweisungen (siehe unten).

Stellen Sie sich vor, Sie sind in einem Seminar. Erklären Sie Ihren Kollegen/innen die wichtigsten Anweisungen und diskutieren Sie sie mit ihnen.

MACHINE TOOL SAFETY

FOR MAXIMUM SAFETY AROUND MACHINE TOOLS:

1. BEFORE you START a machine, be sure you know what is going to happen, KNOW your MACHINE.

2. Be sure you know how to STOP the machine before you start it. KNOW your MACHINE.

3. MAINTAIN the machine in GOOD OPERATING ORDER. Report unusual conditions or machine malfunctions immediately.

4. Always STOP your MACHINE before REMOVING a finished WORKPIECE from in front of the spindle. Do not place your hands near a rotating tool.

5. Never attempt to perform any cleaning, chip removal or work piece clamping while units are in motion. This is like running a race and someday you may lose the race.

6. If you are assigned an assistant for any reason, both the assistant and the operator have the responsibility of deciding who will be in command of the machine and its controls. Only one person should control the machine. ANYONE ELSE SHOULD STAND CLEAR AND BE VISIBLE TO THE PERSON WHO IS ASSIGNED TO OPERATE THE MACHINE CONTROLS.

7. Remember that your work area may change during the day as material is delivered to and removed from your machine area. Be alert for pinch point and work hazard areas created by workpiece storage.

8. Keep the immediate area clean. Avoid slippery floors, remove debris, remove obstacles, remove chips, etc.
Chips that are allowed to accumulate in the area in which you must walk are a hazard that can cause you to fall or slip against the machine or its controls.

| Kopiervorlage | Unit 16 |

3
Sehen Sie sich die Sicherheitsanweisungen (siehe unter 2) genau an und diskutieren Sie sie unter Berücksichtigung der folgenden Punkte:

a. Do you think the instructions are useful?

b. Which instructions do you consider most useful and which ones do you think are possibly unnecessary? Give reasons.

c. What kind of accidents happen most in factories and why?

d. How can accidents be avoided?

e. Which actions should be taken when an accident has happened?

17 A helping hand (1)

Lernstoffübersicht – Lehr- und Arbeitsbuch
Schwerpunkte

Themen / Inhalte	Grammatik / Übungen	Situations / Functions
Grundlagen eines Industrieroboters (mit der entsprechenden technischen Zeichnung) und Beschreibung der elementaren Funktionen und Einrichtungen	Ausdrücke mit *do* und *make* in ähnlicher Grundbedeutung *(do business / make a lot of noise)*	Verstehen eines beschreibenden technischen Textes (mit Zeichnungen)
	Schriftliche Übung	Bitten ausdrücken und formulieren / in höflicher Form Anweisungen geben / Leute auffordern (z. B. *Check that, will you?*)
Welche Rolle können Roboter übernehmen?	Struktur- und Vokabelübungen	

Technische Hintergrundinformationen

axis (plural): axes ['æksiːz]): in mathematics, a line of significant reference for a graph or figure, for example x- und y-axes in Cartesian co-ordinates.

payload: 1) the revenue-producing part of a cargo; 2) the passengers, mail, and cargo in an aircraft; 3) in rockets and satellites, the data-collecting and transmitting equipment; 4) in manned spacecraft, the personnel, life-support systems, and equipment necessary to accomplish missions *(= Nutzlast)*.

servomechanism: device that uses a small amount of power to control the activity of a much more powerful device (e.g. as in power-assisted steering on a motor vehicle).

servo motors: electric or hydraulic motors in an automatic control system (e.g. the operation of a large valve by a governor *[= Regler]* of small power).

Schlüssel zu den Übungen im Lehrbuch

1. a. high payload robot b. cast aluminium c. they require no adjustment and are easy to fit and remove d. six

2. Erstellen eines Artikels zum Thema „Roboter"

3. a. make b. make c. do d. take e. Make f. Do g. do h. make i. take j. do k. Make

4. Hörverständnisübung – vergleiche Tapescript im Anhang S. 118

5. Diskussion über Industrieroboter und Automatisierung

Anmerkungen und Schlüssel zu den Kopiervorlagen

2. Beispiele:
   machine tools / welding / spray painting / chip production / plastics processing / nuclear reactors

3. a. do *(Tut mir leid, aber bei dieser Besprechung werden Sie ohne Zigaretten auskommen müssen.)* b. making *(Er verdiente 60 Dollar die Stunde, als er in New York war.)* c. made *(Ihr Haus war aus Ziegelsteinen gebaut.)* d. made *(Um die Rechnung zu begleichen, stellte sie einen Scheck in Höhe von $800 aus.)* e. do *(Was haben Sie mit den Werkzeugen gemacht?)* f. doing *(Was macht sie gerade?)* g. made *(Nun, sie hat in der Tat gestern die falsche Entscheidung gefällt.)* h. do *(Was wollen Sie machen, wenn Sie die technische Hochschule verlassen?)*

4. The merchant has to make several different crossings to get his things safely to the other side:
   a. Cross with goat – return empty handed;
   b. cross with fox – bring back the goat;
   c. cross with cabbage – come back empty handed;
   d. cross with goat.

Kopiervorlage — Unit 17

1
Zusätzlicher Text / Diktat:

The Stäubli "Neater" is a standard robot product combining the robotic expertise of Stäubli Unimation with the unique requirements of the nuclear industry, represented by Harwell Laboratory and their Engineering Sciences Division. The "Neater" is a modern robot that can do a number of well-defined and repetitive tasks which demand accurate control under difficult and dangerous conditions. The "Neater" robot incorporates seals and radiation tolerant components, thus making it ideally suited to nuclear application areas such as waste management, reprocessing, and fuel production. Together with the electronic Harwell controller, the "Neater" robot can also be used with a remote control. It uses the best in established robot control technology and reduces the costs associated with operations such as waste management.

2
Wortfelder (Gruppenarbeit)
Jede Gruppe versucht, die leeren Felder mit einem passenden Begriff aus dem Wortfeldbereich zu füllen. Anschließend vergleichen die einzelnen Gruppen ihre Ergebnisse und beschreiben die Tätigkeiten, die die Roboter in den angegebenen Gebieten ausführen können.

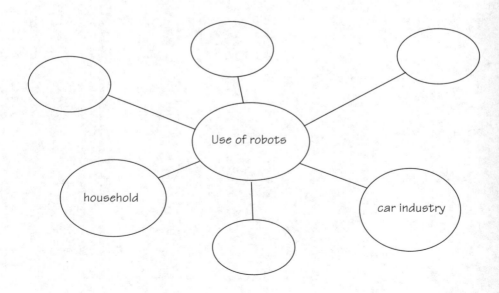

| Kopiervorlage | Unit 17 |

3
Setzen Sie die richtige Form von *do* oder *make* ein und übersetzen Sie die Sätze:

a. Well, I'm sorry, but you'll have to _____ without cigarettes on this meeting.

b. He was _____ 60 dollars an hour when he was in New York.

c. Their house was _____ of brick.

d. She _____ a cheque out for $800 to pay the bill.

e. What did you _____ with the tools?

f. What is she _____?

g. Well, as a matter of fact, she _____ the wrong decision yesterday.

h. What do you want to _____ when you leave technical college?

4
... and a brain teaser:

Many years ago there was a merchant who had to cross a river by boat. There was a rule in the area where he lived stating that he could take only one object at a time in his boat He had a cabbage, a goat and a fox. So on each of his trips he had to leave two things together on one side of the river.

And that's where the problems began: He could not leave the goat with the cabbage because the goat would eat it. And he could not leave the fox and the goat because the fox would kill the goat. How can he take all his things safely to the other side of the river?

18 A helping hand (2)

Lernstoffübersicht – Lehr- und Arbeitsbuch
Schwerpunkte

Themen / Inhalte	Grammatik / Übungen	Situations / Functions
Zweiter Teil der Einführung in die Verwendung und Konstruktion von Industrierobotern (hier speziell) das CS-Steuergerät)	Erster Teil der kurzen Einführung in den Komplex -*ing form*, hier mit Ausdrücken wie z. B. *Have you done the cleaning? / I hate getting up early)*	Verstehen einer technischen Erläuterung (Steuereinheit eines Industrieroboters)
		Im Museum (Science Museum in London) – Change and the chemical industry
Zukünftige Entwicklungen technischer Art *(What will the future bring???)* – Diskussion/Group work	Strukturübungen (besonders -*ing form*)	
		Bitten ausdrücken

Technische Hintergrundinformationen

controller: an instrument that automatically and continuously measures the value of a variable quantity or condition and then acts on the controlled equipment to correct devia-tions from the desired preset value.

deadman's switch (also: deadman's handle): 1) a form of switch or handle commonly used on the controllers of electric vehicles: it is designed so that if the driver releases his or her pressure on the switch or handle, owing to sudden illness or other causes, the current is cut off and the brakes are applied; 2) in electronics, an electrical switch that activ-ates some function if it is turned off *(= Totmannfunktion, Totmannkopf; Sicherheitsschaltung).*

ergonomics: this science is concerned with the relationship between human beings and the machines or equipment they use; it involves the application of physiological, anatomical and psychological data to the design of working systems *(= Ergonomie).*

heat-exchanger: a device that employs two separate streams of fluid (gas or liquid) for heating or cooling one of them, for example a car radiator uses air flow to cool water *(= Wärmetauscher).*

port: in computing, the port is the point at which signals from peripheral equipment enter the computer *(= Port, Anschluß, Ausgang).*

Schlüssel zu den Übungen im Lehrbuch

1. Hörverständnis – vergleiche Tapescript im Anhang S. 118

2. a. False; Peter, Manfred and Jane are having breakfast. b. False c. True d. True e. False

3. a. He keeps making mistakes all the time. b. She enjoys working with the new CAD software. c. They look forward to using the new camcorder during their holiday in Canada. d. They hate having to redesign all the computer terminals. e. Have you finished reading the specifications of the RS 156 Industrial Robot? f. She looks forward to meeting her English friend at the conference next week. g. The engineers hate going to that meeting every Monday. h. You have to keep trying. i. Your car needs washing. j. He usually goes swimming on Sundays. k. Do you do the checking? l. I have to finish writing the accident report first. m. She looks forward to spending some time in Canada.

4. Diskussion über die Welt im Jahr 2030

5. a. borrow ... means   b. changing ... wonder   c. use ... works   d. seeing e. Producing ... was

Anmerkungen und Schlüssel zu den Kopiervorlagen

2. a. shouldn't   b. might   c. should   d. might   e. should   f. should

3. a. First they had some difficulties but then they went on writing the technical report. b. He keeps talking about the new robots although ... c. He admitted that he had got a ticket for speeding yesterday. d. She suggested we should go ...

4. a. processing   b. processing   c. production   d. production   e. display   f. display

5. Area of section: 1,050 mm^2

Kopiervorlage — Unit 18

1
Zusätzlicher Text / Diktat:

Human factors engineering – also known as ergonomics – is the application of scientific knowledge about human behaviour to design. Although originally concerned with the design of equipment used at work, its techniques can be applied to any product used by people. The products may be hand-tools, or ticket barriers, or the working environment in an office. Ergonomics is of growing importance in the design of consumer products, especially where users with special requirements are involved, such as children or disabled people. But it is not just machinery that benefits from attention to ergonomics – increasingly it is being used to make computer software more user friendly.

For many products, particularly innovative ones, it is not easy to discover how people will use them or what aspects of human behaviour are relevant to their design. One of the most important aspects of human factors, therefore, is predicting user behaviour and building it into successful products.

For example, it is common practice in the software industry to give users the prompt "press any key to continue". No doubt this seemed helpful and friendly to the software designer. After all, he was not asking the user to show specific keying skill by finding a particular key. However, what the designers failed to predict was that by presenting users with a choice, for no apparent reason and without any obvious basis for making the choice, they disrupted the thinking process. Worse than that, they created doubt and suspicion in the user's mind that the designer did not really mean "any key". Indeed, software retailers report having been phoned by users to ask which key is the "any key" as it does not appear on their keyboard.

2
Might oder *should/shouldn't?*

a. You _____ do that – it's dangerous.

b. If I can save enough money, I _____ come and visit you in Canada next year.

c. If you see anything unusual, you _____ call the police.

d. Don't touch that wire – it _____ be dangerous!

e. I think you _____ finish this report as soon as possible.

f. If you ask me, I think things like that _____ be forbidden!

Kopiervorlage — Unit 18

3
Ändern Sie die Sätze um, indem Sie eines der folgenden Wörter benutzen, ohne dabei den Inhalt zu verändern.

admit / go on / keep / suggest

a. First they had some difficulties but then they continued to write the technical report.

b. He always talks about the new robots although nobody is interested in them any longer.

c. He said he got a ticket for speeding yesterday.

d. She said we should go to the boat exhibition in February.

4
Welches Wort gehört in die Mitte?

display / processing / production

a. central [　　　　] unit

b. data [　　　　] speed

c. mechanical [　　　　] process

d. textile [　　　　] areas

e. visual [　　　　] terminal

f. visual [　　　　] unit

5
... and a bit of maths:

Find the area of the section shown on the right (in mm).

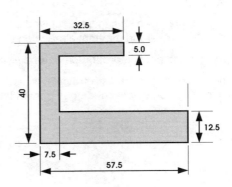

19 Bits and bytes: PROCEDE for Windows

Lernstoffübersicht – Lehr- und Arbeitsbuch
Schwerpunkte

Themen / Inhalte	Grammatik / Übungen	Situations / Functions
Vorstellung eines Computerprogramms, das zusammen mit CAD-Programmen verwendet werden kann (Originaltext aus einer Firmenbroschüre mit den entsprechenden Diagrammen und Zeichnungen) / Diskussion über Computer	Zweiter Teil der Erläuterungen zum Thema -*ing form*, hier mit den Bedeutungsunterschieden zwischen den Formen (z. B. *I remember writing ... / I must remember to write ...*)	Einarbeiten in einen relativ anspruchsvollen technischen Text (Programmbeschreibung)
	Sprechübungen	Beschreibung von Gegenständen, Zuständen, Vorgängen und Materialien (z. B. *... liable to ...*)

Technische Hintergrundinformationen

<u>auxiliary program:</u> extra (or specialized) program that can work with a main program *(= Hilfsprogramm)*.

<u>drag:</u> to move a mouse with the control key pressed, so that an image moves on the screen (to the position wanted) *(= „ziehen")*.

<u>flowsheet:</u> chart which shows the arrangement of steps in a process or program *(= Flußdiagramm)*.

<u>library</u> –> <u>symbol table</u>

<u>logic chart:</u> graphical representation of the logic design; it shows the existence of functional elements and the paths by which they interact with one another *(= Logikdiagramm)*.

<u>pull-down menu:</u> menu which can be displayed on screen at any time by pressing a key, usually displayed over the material already on screen *(= Pull-Down-Menü)*.

<u>scale:</u> to lower or increase in proportion or size *(= skalieren)*.

<u>symbol table</u> (also: <u>library</u>): a list of available tables, names, or symbols (for example, electric circuit symbols), which may be copied into an existing drawing *(= Bibliothek)*.

Schlüssel zu den Übungen im Lehrbuch

1. Diskussion über CAD/CAM
2. Zusammenfassen eines Textes
3. Hörverständnisübung – vergleiche Tapescript im Anhang S. 119
4. a. to get   b. to use   c. sending   d. making   e. to tell   f. meeting   g. to inform
5. Bildgesteuerte Vorgangsbeschreibung
6. Hörverständnisübung – vergleiche Tapescript im Anhang S. 120
7. Diskussion über neue Technologien

Anmerkungen und Schlüssel zu den Kopiervorlagen

2. a. carrying   b. numerical   c. controlled = CNC   d. rail   e. power   f. manufacturing = rpm
3. provides ... developed ... call up ... using ... appears ... accept ... return ... add
4. a. Die Erarbeitung der Lösung wird leichter, wenn man die Schiffe (A, B, C und D) aus Karton ausschneidet und dann zwischen gezeichneten Linien hin und her bewegt.

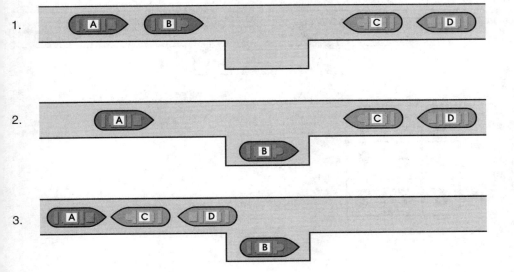

Kopiervorlage Unit 19

4.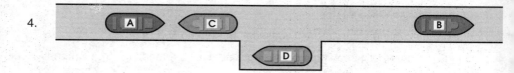

5.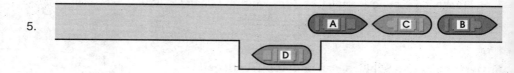

6.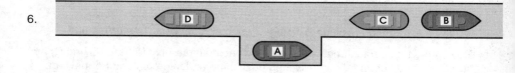

7.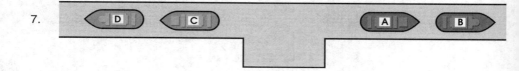

b.

8	3	4
1	5	9
6	7	2

Kopiervorlage   Unit 19

1
Zusätzlicher Text / Diktat

Network software has made setting up a LAN easier than ever, but the wide choice of hardware such as adapter cards and cables makes assembling a network a very detailed task. So, understanding the basic network concepts and identifying the pieces of hardware necessary to implement a LAN is the key, if your network implementation is going to be successful. The concept behind every network is the interconnection of two or more PCs with a cable. The type of cable used and the method of connecting the PC to it vary between types of networks, but the idea remains the same. There are networks available which will allow you to connect PCs using their serial ports, but these are only suitable for the most basic of requirements, and performance is naturally very limited. For serious network use, you need an adapter card which is installed in a free slot in your PC.

2
Welches Wort gehört in die Mitte?

Von oben nach unten gelesen ergeben die ersten drei Anfangsbuchstaben die Abkürzung von *computer numerical control* und die Anfangsbuchstaben der letzten drei Wörter die Abkürzung für *revolutions per minute*:

a. load ⎕⎕⎕⎕⎕ capacity

b. computerized ⎕⎕⎕⎕⎕ control

c. numerically ⎕⎕⎕⎕⎕ machines

d. light ⎕⎕⎕⎕⎕ transit

e. hydraulic ⎕⎕⎕⎕⎕ supply

f. flexible ⎕⎕⎕⎕⎕ systems

Kopiervorlage   Unit 19

3
Setzen Sie die folgenden Wörter in der richtigen Form in die Lücken ein:

accept / add / appear / call up / develop / provide / return / use

SpecSht _____ easy access to a library of industry standard data specification sheets which have been _____ by experienced process engineers. You can _____ a data sheet associated with a particular symbol at any time from *FloSheet* _____ the mouse. The data sheet instantly _____ ready to _____ input. From *FloSheet* you can _____ to your data sheet and _____ more data for each symbol.

4
... and TWO brain teasers:

a. On a narrow canal there are four barges – A, B, C and D (see below). Two barges are going in one direction and two in the other. It is impossible for them to pass, because the canal is too narrow. However, the engineers have built a place where one barge can fit. How then, making use of this space, can all the barges follow their route? Important note: the barges can reverse as well as go forward.

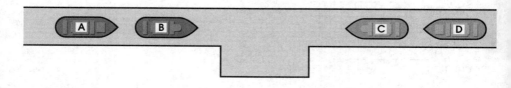

b. In a square (see figure on the right) divided into nine parts, put th e numbers 1, 2, 3, 4, 5, 6, 7, 8 and 9 in such a way that whether you add them horizontally, vertically or diagonally your total will always be 15. You cannot put one of the numbers twice and you must use all the numbers from one to nine.

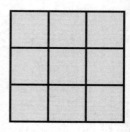

20 Bits and bytes: Images and cyberspace

Lernstoffübersicht – Lehr- und Arbeitsbuch
Schwerpunkte

Themen / Inhalte	Grammatik / Übungen	Situations / Functions
Vorstellung einer Entwicklung, die an Bedeutung gewinnen wird: *Virtual Reality*	Ausdrücke mit *mind* (z. B. *change one's mind / never mind / I don't mind*)	Im Museum (Science Museum in London)
	Leseverstehen	Erarbeiten eines anspruchsvollen technischen Textes
Darstellung eines Bildbearbeitungsprogramms (mit dem entsprechenden Vokabular) und Beschreibung der Vorgänge	Hörverständnis	Ausdruck von Besitz (Zugehörigkeit / Eigenschaften: *... it is comprised of ...*)
	Diskussion (*Virtual Reality / Leisure*)	

Technische Hintergrundinformationen

<u>algorithm:</u> a set of well-defined rules for the solution of a problem in a finite number of steps; the term is commonly used in the context of computer programming *(= Algorithmus)*

<u>algorithm translation:</u> step-by-step computerized method of translating one programming language into another.

<u>algorithmic language:</u> a language in which a procedure or scheme of calculations can be expressed accurately.

<u>customize:</u> to modify a system or program to the customer's requirements *(= auf den Kundenbedarf zuschneiden).*

<u>cyberspace:</u> the world of virtual reality.

<u>cybernetics:</u> the study of control and communications in complex electronic systems and in human beings and animals *(= Kybernetik).*

<u>macro:</u> program routine or block of instructions identified by a single label: a single macro instruction can produce several lines of machine-language code; if, for example, the programmer writes "READ FILE" the translating software will automatically provide a detailed series of previously prepared machine-language instructions which can copy a record into primary storage from the file of data being read by the input device, thus relieving the programmer of the task of writing an instruction for every machine operation performed.

<u>menu-driven software:</u> programs where commands or options are selected from a menu *(= menügesteuerte Software).*

ruggedize: to strengthen a machine for better resistance to wear, stress, and abuse; a ruggedized computer *(= ein für erschwerte Umweltbedingungen gebauter Computer).*

spreadsheet: 1) program for calculations with several columns of numbers; 2) printout of calculations *(= Spreadsheet, Tabellenkalkulation, Arbeitsblatt).*

Zum besseren Verständnis der in Unit 20 vorgestellten Programmteile **Image Analyst** dient folgender Auszug aus dem Prospekt:

"Image Analyst is a menu-driven image processing and analysis software package that runs on the Macintosh family of computers. This interface allows you to quickly apply the latest image processing algorithms without the complexities of traditional programming. It is designed to process both live video and stored image files, and to extract quantitative data. Image Analyst comes with an extensive set of interactive image examination tools, image processing routines, and powerful image analysis options ...
Collections of image processing and analysis operations on multiple regions of interest can be saved and executed as user-defined sequences. Now you can easily assemble a sequence of instructions to automatically enhance feature appearance; count objects; determine density, shape, size, position, and movement; perform object feature extraction; conduct textural analysis; and much more—all this with unequaled repeatability.
Image Analyst applications can be found in science, medicine, defense, research, and industry ..."

Schlüssel zu den Übungen im Lehrbuch

1. Hörverständnis und Diskussion über *Virtual Reality*

2. a. computer   b. printer   c. scanner   d. fax

3. Hörverständnisübung – vergleiche Tapescript im Anhang S. 121

4. a. – f. = Do you mind if I ...?

5. Diskussion über Freizeitaktivitäten

6. a. Do you mind opening the window? b. Please keep in mind what I told you. c. Do you mind if I open the window? d. I don't mind the rain. e. ... Did you change your mind? f. ... to my mind. g. ... to keep my mind on my work. h. She doesn't mind working with computers, but she does mind bad monitors. i. I'm still searching my mind for her name.

7. a. technique   b. tough   c. technically advanced   d. standardized unit   e. better   f. spreadsheet   g. special characteristics

8. Fragen zum Text

Anmerkungen und Schlüssel zu den Kopiervorlagen

2. Beispiele:
   distribution systems / conveyor systems / control systems / systems analyst / systems analysis / systems design / systems software

3. Offene Kommunikationsübung (ballistics = the study of the movement of objects that are shot or thrown through the air / seismography = having to do with the recording of the period, extent and direction of the vibrations of an earthquake)

4. Offene Kommunikationsübung

5. 1. = a. / 2. = b. / 3. = c. / 4. = c. / 5. = a. / 6 = b.

Kopiervorlage — Unit 20

1
Zusätzlicher Text / Diktat

The invention of the telephone as a practical instrument dates from 1876 when Alexander Graham Bell applied for his first Patent in the United States. Bell had been born in Scotland but had emigrated with his parents to America and, following his father, had taken up the profession which we should now call speech therapy.

He knew that sound consisted of pressure waves in the air and that the different notes were really due to the different frequencies of vibration. Early in the 1870's he conceived the idea that it might be possible to send a number of telegraph messages simultaneously along the same pair of wires by making use of different frequencies. His experiments were unsuccessful – indeed the principle was not applied successfully until many years later – but they led him, almost by accident, to the transmission of human speech.

At first he used the same form of instrument both as transmitter and receiver. As a receiver it was an efficient device and, in fact, it has remained almost unchanged in principle to the present day; as a transmitter, however, it was inefficent. Fortunately the invention of the carbon microphone by Hughes, Edison, Blake and others supplied the deficiency and by the early 1880's the telephone had become a practical instrument.

The first telephone exchange in London was opened at No. 36 Coleman Street in August 1879. Initially there were only ten subscribers but by 1884 there were about 3,800 in London and about 9,000 throughout the rest of the country.

2
Wortfelder (Gruppenarbeit)

Jede Gruppe versucht, die leeren Felder mit einem passenden Begriff aus dem Wortfeldbereich zu füllen. Anschließend vergleichen die einzelnen Gruppen ihre Ergebnisse.

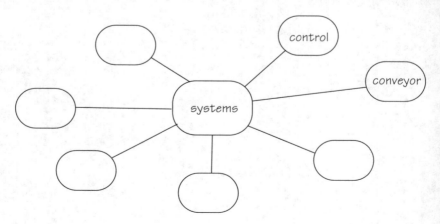

Kopiervorlage — Unit 20

3
Gruppenarbeit.

Jede Gruppe sucht sich jeweils einen Begriff unter *Application* und einen Begriff unter *Industries* aus und stellt zunächst schriftlich die Anwendungsgebiete eines Computers in dem von ihnen gewählten Bereich auf.

Anschließend berichten die Gruppen über ihre Ergebnisse und diskutieren sie.

APPLICATIONS	INDUSTRIES
• Process Monitoring	• Manufacturing
• Data Acquisition	• Laboratory
• Remote Interface	• Oceanography
• Machine Control	• Oil Exploration
• Data Collection	• Medical
• Diagnostics	• Ballistics
• Event Control	• Fire Fighting
• Machine Vision	• Military
• Measurement	• Seismography
• Analysis	• Aerospace

4
Diskutieren Sie die folgenden Beispiele.

Introducing Virtual Reality. In which way can architects, engineers, salespeople or people in other professions profit from VR? Find other examples.

With VR, engineers can, for example, not only visualise an engine, they can walk round it, pick up pipes, undo bolts and practice two-handed maintenance – on something that does not yet exist.

With VR, retail outlets can show customers how a table or chair, at present standing on the showroom floor, might fit in their living room.

| Kopiervorlage | Unit 20 |

5
... and a final quiz:

1. An electric charge can be produced by rubbing. This is because ...
   a. electrons are rubbed off one surface onto the other.
   b. friction causes heat.
   c. one of the substances is wool.
   d. protons are rubbed off one surface onto the other.

2. Substances expand when heated because ...
   a. the molecules get bigger as they vibrate faster.
   b. the space between molecules gets bigger as they vibrate faster.
   c. they have more energy as they vibrate faster.

3. The time taken for light to reach us from the sun is ...
   a. 8.5 days.
   b. 8.5 hours.
   c. 8.5 minutes.
   d. 8.5 seconds.

4. The smallest planet in the Solar System is ...
   a. Earth.
   b. Venus.
   c. Mercury.

5. The magnetic pole of the Earth is not the geographic North Pole but is somewhere in ...
   a. Canada.
   b. Iceland.
   c. Norway.
   d. Siberia.

6. Plastics are substances with ...
   a. a strong crystal structure.
   b. long tangled molecules.
   c. small slippery molecules.

Testing Your Language — Part Two

A. Listening comprehension
   1. True
   2. False (only the chamber)
   3. True
   4. True
   5. True
   6. True
   7. True
   8. False
   9. True

B. Listening comprehension
   Text one = C
   Text two = G
   Text three = B

C. Reading comprehension
   1. = b.
   2. = a.
   3. = b.
   4. = a.
   5. = a.
   6. = b.
   7. = b.
   8. = b.
   9. = b.

D. Reading comprehension
   1. = d.
   2. = d.
   3. = a.
   4. = c.

Tapescripts

UNIT 1, Exercise 3

<u>Making an appointment</u>

Audrey: I'd like to make an appointment for the interview, please – you have my written application.
Ms Penrose: Oh yes, I know – Bell, Audrey Bell. Would ten o'clock on Tuesday be convenient? Here in our Coventry office.
Audrey: Yes, that would be fine.
Ms Penrose: OK – Tuesday, ten ...
Audrey: Exactly where is your office? I sent my application to your London office, you know.
Ms Penrose: Oh yes, I see. Well, we're on Spencer Avenue, opposite Spencer Park. It's a big red building with a large car park in front – you can't miss it, really ...

UNIT 1, Exercise 7

This is message a.:
"Hello, this is John Hamilton speaking – International Machine Tools. Could you give a message to Lisa Miller – I wasn't able to get through to her. Tell her that the milling machine she ordered left our factory this morning. She can expect delivery tomorrow, I think. If there are any further questions, she can reach me this afternoon – my number is 886-22971. Thank you. Goodbye."

Here is message b.:
"Hello, InterElectronics here, Mary Rosewall speaking. I wonder if you could give Frank Slide a message about the order number M/6-94. Tell him we're very sorry but we can't deliver before Monday. Please tell him to call me back tomorrow morning. – I must know if he still wants the 20 modems. Thank you. Goodbye."
This is the end of message b.

UNIT 2, Exercise 1

You're going to hear two telephone conversations.

This is telephone conversation a.:

Switchboard: Aldridge Motors Service, good morning.
Luke Taylor: Hello, ... er ... it's Luke Taylor here. Could I speak to Mr Roberts, please?
Switchboard: Just a moment, I'll see if he's in ... I'll put you through to his office.
Secretary: Hello, Mr Robert's office.

Luke Taylor:	Could I speak to Mr Roberts, please?
Secretary:	I'm very sorry, but he's out at lunch. Can I help you, perhaps?
Luke Taylor:	Well, yes ... er ... maybe you can. Could you ask him to call me back? Today if possible – before 3 pm ... or ... yes, any time tomorrow. He's got several cars from our fleet – for servicing, you know.
Secretary:	Yes, certainly. Who's calling, please?
Luke Taylor:	This is Luke Taylor, of Exec International.
Secretary:	Luke Taylor ... yes. And can I take your number, please?
Luke Taylor:	Yes, of course – it's 639 4427.
Secretary:	So ... that's 639 4437.
Luke Taylor:	No – 27 – not 37 – 4427.
Secretary:	Oh, sorry – 27 – OK. Well, Mr Taylor, I'll ask Mr Roberts to call you as soon as he comes back to the officce.
Luke Taylor:	Thank you very much. Goodbye.
Secretary:	Goodbye, Mr Taylor.

That was telephone conversation a. Now you're going to hear ...
... telephone conversation b.:

Switchboard:	CAD Engineering, good afternoon.
Adam Jonson:	This is Adam Jonson, of Buckland Motors Limited. I'd like to speak to Mr Michael Jones, please – he's in the design department, I think, design and testing.
Switchboard:	Michael Jones ... oh, I'm sorry, he isn't in today. He has the flu, in fact, he won't be in for the next couple of days.
Adam Jonson:	Oh, I'm sorry to hear that. Is there anybody else I could talk to? In the design department, I mean. Perhaps Mr Davies – is he there?
Switchboard:	Let me see ... John Davies ... yes, he should be in. I'll put you through.
John Davies:	Davies speaking.
Adam Jonson:	Hello, John. This is Adam Jonson –
John Davies:	Oh, hello Adam! Is there anything I can do for you?
Adam Jonson:	Well, there's a little problem with the material Michael Jones sent us – the CAD printouts and spreadsheets, you know ...
John Davies:	Yes, I know. Anything wrong?
Adam Jonson:	No no, they're fine, it's just that one spreadsheet seems to be missing – spreadsheet 663, you know, and we need it urgently.
John Davies:	That shouldn't be a problem ... let me see ... yes, I've got his things here on the desk ... ah, yes, here it is – 663!
Adam Jonson:	Could you fax it to me right away?
John Davies:	Yes, certainly, no problem. I can't wait to try out my brand-new fax machine.
Adam Jonson:	Fine. Thanks a lot for your help. Bye-bye.
John Davies:	Bye-bye.

UNIT 2, Exercise 10

<u>At the Coventry office</u>

Receptionist: Good morning. May I help you?
Audrey: Yes. Good morning. My name is Bell, Audrey Bell. I have an appointment at ten with Ms Penrose – Personnel Department, I think.
Receptionist: For a job interview?
Audrey: Yes.
Receptionist: Have a seat.
Audrey: Thank you.
Receptionist: Now let me see ... ah yes, here we are ... Audrey Bell ... ten a.m. You can go right in, I think – room twelve, right around the corner. There's a large yellow door on the left. I'll tell her that you're on the way.
Audrey: Thank you.

UNIT 3, Exercise 2

<u>The job interview (1)</u>

Ms Penrose: Yes, come in.
Audrey: Good morning, Ms Penrose.
Ms Penrose: Yes – You're Ms Bell, aren't you – Audrey Bell?
Audrey: Yes, that's right.
Ms Penrose: Glad to meet you. Have a seat. Did you have any trouble finding our office?
Audrey: No, not at all. I'm sorry I'm a bit late, but there was an accident on the A44.
Ms Penrose: Oh, that's all right. It's only a few minutes anyway ... well, let's see ... I've got your CV here – looks very good, by the way – and I'd like to ask you a few questions ...
Audrey: Yes, certainly ....
Ms Penrose: Particularly about your experience with CIM ...
Audrey: I did a CIM course at College, in fact.

UNIT 3, Exercise 3

The population of the world continues to grow all the time, and towns and cities are expading. That's why more and more money will have to be spent on new rapid transit systems in the future.

Consequently, companies in the transportation field are trying to convince transport authorities and politicians of the advantages of their own special systems. This is not always easy, and there is quite a lot of competition. The advantages emphasized by companies hoping to sell their systems range from lightweight construction, low noise and vibration, to lack of emission fumes. The number of people a system can handle within a short period of time is also of importance.

Maglev systems, the manufacturers say, are much lighter and smaller than conventional systems because there is no electrical equipment in the carriages. They consume seventy percent less energy than conventional systems, and are easy to maintain. Furthermore, and this should not be forgotten, they are said to be very safe – the magnets keep the carriages just above the track even if the motors fail. Ice is no problem either, because there is no friction between the train and the track.

UNIT 4, Exercise 4

Text a.

A simple, cheap and effective way of increasing the efficiency of radiators located on outside walls is to fix aluminium foil on the wall behind the radiator. This reflects heat back into the room that would otherwise be lost through the outside wall.

Text b.

You should also think about installing a shower. Showers use less hot water than baths.

Text c.

When installing electric storage radiators, consider models which can be controlled by an outside temperature sensor. This automatically adjusts the amount of heat stored overnight according to the external temperature.

Text d.

Pipes leading from the hot water tank and all central heating pipes that are hidden under floors should be insulated. The pipe insulation should have a thickness of 13 mm or more.

Text e.

Heat pumps and solar panels may play an important role in the future, but at the present stage of development they may be too expensive for some houses.

UNIT 4, Exercise 6

The job interview (2)

Ms Penrose: Most of our extrusion processes are computer controlled, so that's what you'll be working on most of the time.
Audrey: That's fine with me – I like working with computers.
Ms Penrose: That's very good – our managers are not so fond of computers.
Audrey: What sort of things do you produce?
Ms Penrose: Mostly extruded components, but we also do some finishing – anodising, for example – window and door frames, shower cubicles, etc.
Audrey: I would very much like to have a look at the shop floor.
Ms Penrose: No problem – I'm sure Calvin Mill, our Chief Engineer, will be happy to show you around ...

UNIT 5, Exercise 1

There are lots of things people have to pay for in their communities – local taxes, charges for refuse collection, rents for council houses and flats, garages, or allotment gardens. Or maybe even speeding tickets.
By automating the accounting and recording process, the Westinghouse Automatic Payment Machine (APM) shown here offers you the opportunity to do all these things without having to go to a post office or bank. The machine is located at a convenient place, and it accepts coins, notes, and even cheques. To start it, you just insert a special service card you get from your local authority ...

UNIT 5, Exercise 4

The job interview (3)

Ms Penrose: Well, back to the job. When do you think you could start work.
Audrey: I'm free at the moment – I finished College last month, as you know ...
Ms Penrose: We would like to have you as soon as possible.
Audrey: I could start next week, if that's all right ...
Ms Penrose: Fine, yes – I think you can have the job.
Audrey: Thank you!
Ms Penrose: Don't thank me before you see what it involves ...
Audrey: Oh, I think I'll be able to manage.
Ms Penrose: I hope you don't mind doing a bit of overtime – rush orders and so on, you know.
Audrey: That's okay if it's not too often.

UNIT 6, Exercise 1

Your're now going to hear ...

.... text a.

The components are taken to a higher level and automatically transferred to the second conveyor for transportation through an electrophoretic paint plant. This circuit operates at a much slower speed of 1.9 metre/min. Any empty carriers automatically by-pass the paint line conveyor. TI Cox plans to link the two Siemens PLCs that control the conveyors and paint plant. This would give them total management control over the whole process, plus detailed infomation which could lead to further cost-quality improvements.

You have just heard text a. Now you're going to hear ...

... text b.

The system is installed at TI Cox's new Nottingham plant, which produces seats and seat mechanisms for such manufacturers as Rolls Royce, Austin Rover, Jaguar, Saab and Volvo. Both plant and conveyor were designed to handle the combined production of two former factories, streamlining production while maintaining the optimum level of quality. The circuit collects seat components from each of eleven manufacturing cells, where they are loaded manually onto special carriers. The conveyor circulates at 7.6 metre/min and the carriers are pre-coded to identify the manufacturing cell involved.

This is the end of exercise 1.

UNIT 6, Exercise 4

A look at the shop floor

Calvin Mill:	Do you have any experience with aluminium products?
Audrey:	No, not really.
Calvin Mill:	Well, that's no problem – it's not so difficult if you have the basic knowledge. This here, you see, is our biggest extrusion press. It's not exactly new but it works all right.
Audrey:	But this press is not computer-controlled, is it?
Calvin Mill:	No, not this press, but the whole manufacturing process is integrated in the CIM system – we hope everything will be integrated some day.
Audrey:	Yes, I see. Well, I hope I can help a little bit.

UNIT 7, Exercise 3

Back in the office

Ms Penrose:	Did you get all the information you wanted?
Audrey:	Yes, thank you – Mr Hill was very nice. He has helped me a great deal.
Ms Penrose:	Fine. Did he complain about the old press? He usually does.
Audrey:	No, not really. He said it was old, but it seemed to be okay.
Ms Penrose:	He probably didn't want to scare you.
Audrey:	Yes, maybe.
Ms Penrose:	But I think he's right, really – the machine is old. I'm sure we'll have to get a new one soon.
Audrey:	Yes, particularly if we want to get it all integrated in the CIM system.
Ms Penrose:	Yes, definitely. We'll have to get that done by the end of the year.

UNIT 7, Exercise 5

Alice:	Talking about aluminium foil, Henry, I think most of the foil produced goes into the food industry. Is that right?
Henry:	Yes, that's correct. It goes into the food industry, for packaging.
Alice:	Yes, the food industry uses it for packaging. But now it actually looks as though aluminium foil is also being used more and more for industrial products. At least I think so. I remember seeing an article about that the other day.

Henry: Yes, as a matter of fact, aluminium foil is used for the packing of welding rods for steel, to give only one example. Traditionally, welding rods needed to be dried or conditioned just before use because they absorb moisture. Nowadays, they use a special aluminium foil, a kind of laminate, to wrap welding rods.
Alice: That's very interesting indeed. Perhaps you could give me another example.
Henry: Well, let me think ... Oh, yes. As a matter of fact, it's also used for the packaging of moisture-sensitive machine parts to be sent overseas.
Alice: Ah yes ... to keep the moisture out.
Henry: Yes, that's exactly what I mean. Oh – it's already half past nine. I'm afraid I'll have to be off to work now. There's an important meeting at ten – I really have to be there. But it was nice talking to you, Alice. Have a nice day.
Alice: Thanks, you too, and take care!
Henry: Same to you!

UNIT 8, Exercise 1

Linda: I know that aluminium extrusions are used more and more extensively in various fields. There must be a reason for this. Tell us, Mr Bellows, which factors make aluminium an ideal material for industry?
Mr Bellows: Well, the main benefits are that lots of shapes can be extruded. The material is lightweight and yet strong and durable, you need less maintenance, and it looks good. Furthermore, there's a wide range of attractive finishes which are also corrosion-resistant. It's an ideal material, as you said. It's strong, light and versatile.
Peter: I see that, but what I'd like to have are some practical examples. I mean, could you tell us about some areas where aluminium extrusions are used?
Mr Bellows: Well, for instance, I know a factory in Ireland which has new conveyors based on an extruded aluminium frame with an anodized finish. This anodized surface, by the way, is almost completely scratch-proof. When they show their customers around the factory, they're always proud to show them their conveyors, and the customers are always surprised about the sophisticated appearance of the conveyors.
Linda: That's very interesting. Can you give some more examples?
Mr Bellows: Yes, packaging – that's another area of the industrial production process in which aluminium has solved a lot of problems. About forty years ago, aluminium beverage cans for soft drinks were still a novelty. Nowadays you see a lot of them – beer cans, for instance. They're pretty common now and you could say that they have gained a dominant role here. I could go on like this for ages, if you don't stop me beforehand ...
Peter: No, go ahead.
Mr Bellows: Think of the car industry. There, aluminium is used from window systems to engine components – there are plans to build 100% aluminium frames for cars. And before I forget to mention it, aluminium extrusions are being used more and more in the aviation industry. About 200,000 tonnes of aluminium is supplied for the manufacture of aircraft every year.

Linda:	200,000 tonnes – that's quite a lot ...
Mr Bellows:	Yes, and about 20,000 tonnes of that come from the UK. The advantages again are that it can be extruded into very complex shapes, and the manufacturing costs are relatively low. And extrusions can be anodized, as I said, or powder-coated in a wide variety of attractive finishes. So you see, aluminium is an ideal material in military and civil aircraft applications ...

UNIT 8, Exercise 4

<u>First day at work</u>

Audrey:	You're Tim – Tim Gilbert, aren't you?
Tim:	Yes, and you must be the newcomer – welcome to the gang.
Audrey:	Thank you.
Tim:	If there's anything you don't know, just ask me.
Audrey:	Yes, thank you, I'll do that. Could you tell me where I can find a fax machine? I have to send a small drawing to a Bristol office – one of the new window profiles, you know.
Tim:	You mean the architect in Bristol? He's always in a hurry, isn't he?
Audrey:	Yes ...
Tim:	Well, the nearest fax is over there, near Reception. There's another one in Mr Mill's office, but I think this one will do.
Audrey:	Thank you. I'll take care of it right away.

UNIT 9, Exercise 1

There are several methods which can be used for joining zinc coated metal parts together. The various types of welding have already been shown, but there are many other choices, such as mechanical fixing.

A wide range of commercially available fasteners provides a practically unlimited choice of joint method and design. For many applications, standard nuts, screws and bolts are still the most efficient and cheapest options.

One group of fasteners is called "compressive fasteners" (figure 2) because these fasteners depend on a squeezing action to bring the fastened components together. Rivets are an example of this group.

A second group is called "threaded fasteners" – these constitute a very large group as, for example, self-tapping screws.

Nowadays, modern integral assembly techniques have been developed that are particularly suitable for use with Galvatite. One of these techniques is called "clinched section" (figure 3); it can be used when box shapes are being formed.

UNIT 9, Exercise 4

Finding a flat in Coventry

Tim: Well, have you settled down? Any problems?
Audrey: Everything's going well, thank you. It does make a difference when you know your way around.
Tim: Yes, quite.
Audrey: The only problem I have doesn't have anything to do with the company.
Tim: And what is it?
Audrey: I'm trying to find a flat.
Tim: Here in Coventry?
Audrey: Yes.
Tim: Have you had a look at the local newspaper?
Audrey: Yes, but I couldn't find anything.
Tim: You'll probably have to go to one of those estate agencies, maybe they can help you.
Audrey: Yes, maybe I'll have to do that, but first I'll ask around the company.

UNIT 10, Exercise 2

Text a.

Sarah Wallace, 23, lives in Swansea, Wales, where she went to college. She left college with a diploma in Scientific and Technical Illustration and is now working for a small company in Birmingham.

"Things were a bit difficult when I left college – there were not many jobs available, you see. If I hadn't looked for a job right away, I'd still be without work. I found it difficult to adjust to a nine-to-five routine, after being used to a school day. But now I get paid and evenings are free from homework. I find it quite easy to live on my salary, although I was surprised that lunches could be so expensive in the city centre. If at all possible, I'd like to open my own office some day and work as a self-employed commercial illustrator."

Text b.

Andrew Tomkins, 24, is a process engineer with the Peter A. Smithfield Engineering Company in Glasgow.

"At college, I was amazed at the amount of work I had to do. It's so completely different – you have to find things out for yourself instead of being told what to do. We had four course units at the beginning, each one with a weekly lecture and some practical training, plus a lab class – it was about eighteen hours a week altogether. And then came all the really difficult things – control systems, mechanics, thermal power, and so on and so on. I'd like to work abroad for a couple of years – in the USA, maybe, or Australia, and after that get a job with a big multinational company."

Text c.

Simon Keen, 22, is a computer applications assistant with a London-based electronics publishing firm. The firm puts the teletext news and information pages on Channel 4.

"I've always been interested in electronics. A couple of years ago, I decided to do a computer-linked training scheme – I could have gone to college but I thought it was better for me to have some direct access to computers. At first, I studied electronics and technical drawing, so I came into computing with a good background which made it a lot easier to get the job. It's a good job, I must say – I've just moved to a new flat in London. Some day, if all goes well, I'd like to start up my own electronics publishing firm."

UNIT 10, Exercise 7

Inviting friends and colleagues

Tim:	Nice place you have here – I'm glad you found the flat you wanted.
Audrey:	Yes, Duncan helped me, you know. His friend was about to move to Edinburgh, so I took his flat.
Duncan:	And that's why I was invited to this housewarming party ...
Audrey:	No, no – I would have invited you anyway.
Tim:	You've been lucky – it's quite difficult to find a decent place.
Mona:	And at a reasonable rent. I'm still trying to find a nice place to live.
Duncan:	Maybe the company can help ...
Tim:	I don't know ...
Mona:	I can ask – I mean there's no harm in asking, is there?
Tim:	You could ask Ms Penrose – it's not her department but she's very helpful.

TESTING YOUR LANGUAGE – PART ONE

B. Listening comprehension

a. Lufthansa has made its surplus capacity at its training facilities in Bremen, Berlin and Frankfurt available for the instruction of staff of other airlines.

b. Courses are provided for the training of pilots and inflight personnel and are available in five languages.

c. The technology is state-of-the-art and ranges from the latest flight simulator to complex computer systems.

d. Lufthansa has extensive experience in pilot training and a lot of crews are undergoing instruction at its training schools in Bremen, Phoenix and Tucson.

C. Listening comprehension

The Sears distribution centre at Solihull near Birmingham has been equipped with a specially designed conveyor system for hanging clothes. It is one of the largest conveyor systems ever built, and it was installed by Conveyors International in just three months. The system consists of a network of areas linked by powered conveyors that transfer the clothes between the sections. Incoming clothes are hung onto trolleys which are directed by a code to the place where they are needed. The details of each trolley and its contents are entered via a local terminal into the main frame computer. The new distribution centre will consist eventually of sixty sections arranged on two levels and having a capacity of about 400,000 clothes. All CI handling systems are specially made to suit each application from a range of modular components, including automated devices. Systems can be operated manually or powered, or a combination of the two, and can incorporate computer control.

UNIT 11, Exercise 1

Catherine: Now, let's see what's on the agenda ... oh yes, this is the most important thing – the designs for the components. I've heard from Luke that there are a few problems.

Luke: Yes, I'm afraid so. The production department would like to see a few changes.

Michael: Yes, we would, as a matter of fact. There are problems in – well, let me show you an example. You see this part here – the fins are too close together, and the ribs here should be smoother, and there should be a bit more space between them. All that would make it much easier to mass produce the parts later on – and cheaper, of course.

Luke: Yes, I see your point. What about these parts here? Are they all right? We've taken extra care to design the rolling edges correctly.

Michael: Yes, they're fine, Luke – that's exactly what I mean. And these round parts here, too – these pipes – you see the drain holes here? That's very well done, I must say.

Catherine: My boss was a bit worried about the corners and edges in these components here, but I think they're all right now, aren't they?

Luke: Yes, they are now – maybe he saw the old drawings. What I am worried about are the slots in these parts here – there are too many sharp edges – they could cause trouble, you know.

Michael: Yes, that will have to be changed ... let's see ... the bends are all right ... there are no blind holes ... yes, seems all right. Well, back to the computer, then – I'll see that we get the changes finished by tomorrow afternoon.

UNIT 11, Exercise 3

<u>Travelling to the plant</u>

Peter:	Very nice of you to give me a lift.
Manfred:	No problem – it's on my way, really.
Peter:	I've only been here for a week, so I really don't know my way around Zurich.
Manfred:	Well, I don't know Zurich very well either – I'm from Austria, as you probably know.
Peter:	Yes – Linz, you said, didn't you?
Manfred:	Yes.
Peter:	But at least you speak the language. The little I know ...
Manfred:	Where are you from in Britain?
Peter:	London, as a matter of fact.
Manfred:	Ah, here we are – that's the end of the autobahn.
Peter:	Which way now?
Manfred:	That's the plant over there – that big grey building with the large windows.

UNIT 12, Exercise 2

<u>At the company car park</u>

Peter:	Seems pretty full – the car park, I mean.
Manfred:	Yes, it usually is. The shop floor people work in five shifts, you know.
Peter:	There's a free space over there, I think, to the left of that old Citroen.
Manfred:	That's a real old-timer!
Peter:	Yes – Watch it! There's a car coming ...
Manfred:	Damn it! We nearly hit that idiot! Must be mad!
Peter:	Phew – that was close.
Manfred:	Well, here we are. Not much room ... well, should be OK.
Peter:	Will I see you at lunch?
Manfred:	I think so. You think you'll have time for lunch on your first day?
Peter:	I hope so.
Manfred:	Well, I wish you luck.
Peter:	Thanks.
Manfred:	See you.
Peter:	See you, Manfred.

UNIT 12, Exercise 4

This is Mr Robert's answer:

Dear Ms Bellingham,

At first sight, it does sound ridiculous to charge $8.46 for a small screw, but let's look at the economics of it. The screw probably costs the dealer a dollar or so, plus – say – another dollar for the telephone call to order it. A typical postage and packing charge on spares is $5. Add tax to that, and you're up to about $7.50. The dealer's profit comes out at about 80 cents.

If you have problems with your camcorder, it's important to keep a few points in mind:

1. Check that there is a mechanical fault and it is not an easily solved problem to do with the battery, tape or dirty recording heads. Most dealers are helpful, but make sure you check out the fault finder page in your user manual.

2. Take your camcorder, plus any packaging and your sales receipt (which should always be kept in a safe place) back to the dealer.

3. Do it immediately. Delays may cause problems – particularly if you have only just bought the camcorder and want it replaced.

4. If the dealer says he or she is waiting for a spare part from the manufacturer, ask the dealer what the spare part is and when it was ordered. Then write to the manufacturer's managing director to complain.

Maybe these points will help you with possible camcorder problems. Remember: Camcorders are extremely complex, and quite a few repair people are afraid of them!

UNIT 13, Exercise 1

The world's waste problem is quickly piling up into a great mess. The average Parisian is said to throw away nearly 900 pounds of trash a year, a Tokyo resident more than 1,000 pounds. And the most serious problem is the United States: the average American throws away more than half a ton of waste in a single year.

When it comes to solving the world's waste management problems, one thing we can't waste is time. While the world keeps throwing away trash, the earth's waste landfills are rapidly filling up. Very soon, half of those in America will be closed, and in a couple of years Tokyo, Japan, is expected to run out of space. In Germany, more than 40,000 landfill sites have already been declared potentially dangerous.

Across the world, countries are working on solutions. Several studies show that Japan now recycles more than 50 % of its trash, incinerates about 30 % and deposits only about 15 % in landfills. Western Europe recycles more than 30 % of its solid waste, and largescale incineration in waste-to-energy facilities is common. In the United States, which recycles about 15 % of its solid waste and incinerates another 15 %, recycling efforts are increasing with more than 1000 recycling collection programs underway and expanding nationwide.

At Amoco Chemical, we believe that recycling has been neglected and should play a more significant role. Everything recyclable should be recycled. Paper and paperboard, metal cans, glass and plastic. Studies indicate that plastics make up about 10 % of the solid waste in the United States by weight, and, when compressed, make up only about 20 % of the volume. Paper and paperboard are about 33 %, while metal and glass are another 20 %, all by weight. Today, many US companies have already developed new techniques to recycle plastics successfully. Recycling is changing millions of pounds of used plastics into a "natural resource" that can be used to produce toys, pipes, ski jackets and sleeping bags, to name just a few of the products.

UNIT 13, Exercise 3

Driving home

Peter:	Well, that's that – the first day's over.
Manfred:	And how did it go?
Peter:	Not too bad, actually.
Manfred:	That's terrific.
Peter:	Bit of trouble getting used to things, of course.
Manfred:	Yes, I can imagine. I still remember my first day.
Peter:	I feel like celebrating a bit. Say, would you like to come along for a drink or two?
Manfred:	Yes, that would be great.
Peter:	Do you know a nice place in Zurich – not too far from where you live, I mean?
Manfred:	Hmm ... yes, I think so ... there's a small pub off Kreuzstrasse – should be OK, I think.
Peter:	Well, why don't we go there?
Manfred:	Fine. I'll park the car in front of my flat – we can walk from there.

UNIT 14, Exercise 2

Switchboard:	Hello, Urban Transport Corporation.
Jessica Reynolds:	Hello. Can I speak to Mr Walker, please? Peter Walker, Personnel Department.
Switchboard:	Yes, who's calling, please?
Jessica Reynolds:	Jessica Reynolds, OMC.
Switchboard:	Oh yes, just a moment, I'll put you through ...
Peter Walker:	Hello, Jessica. Peter here. How are you?
Jessica Reynolds:	Well, personally I'm fine, thank you. There's a problem with one of our train drivers, however –
Peter Walker:	What happened?
Jessica Reynolds:	Well, he's injured his hand – two fingers, in fact.

Peter Walker:	Broken?
Jessica Reynolds:	Yes, that's what the doctor said.
Peter Walker:	Did you call an ambulance?
Jessica Reynolds:	That wasn't necessary – Michael took him to the hospital.
Peter Walker:	I see. That means we'll have to fill in a Preliminary Accident report. Let's see ... ah yes, here is the form. Now, what do we need first? Name ... yes, name and first name.
Jessica Reynolds:	That's Millikan – M – I – L – L – I – K – A – N – Roy Millikan. You got that?
Peter Walker:	Yes, all right. Date – date of accident – that's today?
Jessica Reynolds:	Yes, this morning.
Peter Walker:	All right ...
Jessica Reynolds:	What's next?
Peter Walker:	Time of accident ...
Jessica Reynolds:	About ten thirty this morning.
Peter Walker:	Ten thirty ... OK. Place?
Jessica Reynolds:	Right outside OMC, there's a small car park ...
Peter Walker:	Outside OMC, near car park ... all right. Position? Train driver, you said?
Jessica Reynolds:	Yes, that's right. He's been with us for years, you know.
Peter Walker:	Uh-huh. Type of injury – broken fingers, you said. How did it happen?
Jessica Reynolds:	He slipped on the wet concrete – there's been quite a lot of rain recently.
Peter Walker:	OK – broken fingers, slipped on wet concrete pavement. Is he in hospital?
Jessica Reynolds:	No, they took him to the out-patients department – he's probably on his way home now.
Peter Walker:	All right, you can sign the preliminary report when you're here tomorrow.
Jessica Reynolds:	OK. 'bye now.
Peter Walker:	See you tomorrow. Bye.

UNIT 14, Exercise 3

<u>Conversation at the pub</u>

Peter:	It's my birthday today, too, as a matter of fact.
Manfred:	Congratulations!
Peter:	Thank you. So you see I've got a very good reason to celebrate.
Manfred:	Yes, absolutely.
Peter:	Nice place, this – a bit different, though.
Manfred:	Different from British pubs, you mean?
Peter:	Yes, quite.
Manfred:	I've only been to Britain once, just for a few days only. I'd love to go again.

Peter: Tell me, why don't we go together? My brother lives in London, you know, and he's got plenty of spare rooms.
Manfred: That would be very nice. Must be a big house, your brother's place.
Peter: It's an old house in Richmond – it belonged to our parents, you know.

UNIT 15, Exercise 1

When you are travelling in areas with a very hot climate, always select a parking site where your RV will be shaded during the hottest part of the day. It is also a good idea to cover your windows since this will keep the inside temperature down.
Air conditioners mounted on the roof of your RV are very useful for hot climates. One precaution should be kept in mind for their operation, however: For the proper operation of any motor, especially the motor in an air conditioner, it is important that the line voltage is not too low. Low voltage causes motors to run hotter than they should and their life is therefore shortened. In many campgrounds, the line voltage is unfortunately not as high as it should be, especially when there is a heavy load on it such as many other air conditioners.
The use of an extension cord to supply power to your RV should be avoided since it often causes a drop in your available voltage. Dim lights and a narrowing of your TV picture are indicators of low voltage. It is a good idea to check available voltage with a voltmeter. In the USA, air conditioners are designed to operate properly between 110 and 120 volts. Running them at lower voltages will shorten their life.

UNIT 15, Exercise 3

<u>Planning a trip to London (1)</u>

Manfred: When are you planning to go to London?
Peter: I'm not sure yet – around Easter, maybe.
Manfred: That would be fine with me. I think I can get a few days off then.
Peter: I'm sure Jane would be very happy to see you – Jane's my sister-in-law, you know.
Manfred: And you're sure it won't be any trouble for them – I mean, with two extra people in the house?
Peter: Oh no, not at all. Brian and Jane are very happy when they've got a lot of people around them.
Manfred: They live in Richmond, you said?
Peter: Yes, just a few miles from London. There's a very good Tube connection – no problem getting to London, you know. I'm sure you'll like it.

UNIT 16, Exercise 1

Jerry Burton: Hi, Alice, nice to see you. Take a seat. You wanted to talk to me?
Alice Sherwood: Hi, Jerry. Yes, and I'm afraid it's not a pleasant subject.
Jerry Burton: Not the complaints again?
Alice Sherwood: Well, I'm afraid so. I've just got the sixth complaint, and it's only December 10th.
Jerry Burton: What is it this time?
Alice Sherwood: The air-conditioning unit.
Jerry Burton: Well, I'll get my records ... ah, here they are. It might be a good idea to go over the whole year.
Alice Sherwood: That's exactly what I wanted to do – there's quite a bit of pressure from my boss, you know. He's just seen the figures for October and November ...
Jerry Burton: Five complaints in October ... four in November.
Alice Sherwood: Yes, that's bad enough.
Jerry Burton: Let's see ... January ... three complaints – and one was the fault of the sales department, you remember –
Alice Sherwood: Yes, I know that, Jerry – it's not a question of fault, we've just got to do something about it. You see here ... February and March – eight complaints each month!
Jerry Burton: That's when we introduced the new CNC system – we had quite a few bugs, I must admit.
Alice Sherwood: And then April, May, June – seven, six, seven.
Jerry Burton: But then it went down – you see: July and August only one and two.
Alice Sherwood: Jerry, that's holiday time.
Jerry Burton: OK, I'm sorry – I know it looks bad. September nine complaints – wow! That's when we had that computer crash. A bad month.
Alice Sherwood: Yes, it sure was.
Jerry Burton: Well, I'll tell you what – we'll have an emergency meeting with the production people next week and we'll go through the cases once again. We must find a solution!

UNIT 16, Exercise 5

Planning a trip to London (2)

Manfred: The question is, how do we get to London?
Peter: We could go by car, of course ...
Manfred: Takes a lot of time, doesn't it?
Peter: Yes, quite. Maybe we should fly.
Manfred: That's quite expensive, isn't it?
Peter: Not really, there's a very good discount rate, you know. Swissair, for example – British Airways have it too, I think.
Manfred: Maybe we should ask the Swissair people.

Peter: They must have an office in Zurich.
Manfred: Yes, I'm sure they have.
Peter: We can also call British Airways ...
Manfred: Yes, good idea. We can see who has the better offer.
Peter: OK.

UNIT 17, Exercise 1

Switchboard: Hello, Bristol Robotics.
Tony: Good morning. Can I speak to Jack Miller, please?
Switchboard: Yes, certainly. Who's calling, please?
Tony: Tony Masterson.
Switchboard: Do you know Mr Miller's extension number?
Tony: Extension number? No ... no, I don't think so.
Switchboard: Let me see ... Miller ... you mean John Miller, advertising department?
Tony: No, Jack Miller – engineering, I believe.
Switchboard: Ah yes – here he is – that's 634 – I'll put you through ...
Monica: Monica Stratford speaking.
Tony: Er ... this is Tony Masterson. Actually, I wanted to speak to Jack – Jack Miller.
Monica: I'm sorry but Jack's out at the moment – he's at a conference, as a matter of fact. He won't be back until Monday next week.
Tony: Hm ... that's too bad.
Monica: Perhaps I can help you? I'm his assistant, you know.
Tony: Oh yes – I think we met at that meeting last month – very briefly only.
Monica: Yes, now I remember. You're working for Boxford Steel, aren't you?
Tony: Yes, that's right.
Monica: Well, what can I do for you?
Tony: Well, it's the robots we bought – You know that we bought some RS 156 robots from you last week?
Monica: Yes, I know.
Tony: What I need – it's urgent, really – are some measurements. We'll be getting the controllers next –
Monica: They're already on the way.
Tony: That's good news. What I need are the basic measurements – for planning workshop space, you know.
Monica: Yes, certainly, I'll just get my manual ... ah, here it is. So, what exactly do you need?
Tony: Width, height – that sort of thing.
Monica: Let's see ... yes, height – 1160 mm plus 360 – that's one metre fifty-two centimetres total height.
Tony: One metre fifty-two – fine. And width?
Monica: Total width sixty centimetres. You need the depth, too?
Tony: Yes, please.

Monica:	That's eighty centimetres, but don't forget the additional thirty centimetres distance from wall. That's for the cables, you know – power supply and so on.
Tony:	Yes, fine ... OK. I Think that will do for the moment. Thanks a lot.
Monica:	Glad to help. Is there anything you want me to pass on to Jack?
Tony:	I don't think so ... Ah yes, wait a minute. You could ask him to send me a copy of the detailed installation plan – the whole layout, you know. I don't know where my copy is.
Monica:	OK, I've got that. I'll pass it on to Jack.
Tony:	Fine, thanks again for your help. Bye-bye.
Monica:	Bye, Tony.

UNIT 17, Exercise 4

<u>At Heathrow Airport</u>

Manfred:	Well, here we are at last – pretty smooth flight, wasn't it?
Peter:	Quite, and on time, too.
Manfred:	Swiss precision ...
Peter:	Yes, must be.
Manfred:	Well, how do we go on from here?
Peter:	We'll have to go to Hammersmith first ... there's an underground map over there, let's have a look ... here, you see ...
Manfred:	Piccadilly Line ...
Peter:	Yes, Piccadilly Line to Hammersmith, and then District Line to Richmond.
Manfred:	How long is it going to take?
Peter:	Depends on the connection, of course, but I think not much more than an hour or so.
Manfred:	Fine, let's go then.
Peter:	OK.

UNIT 18, Exercise 1

All Stäubli-Unimation electric robots series RS 156 are equipped with the CS controller capable of operating in the most hostile industrial environments. This controller contains a heat-exchanger and air filtering equipment (protection class IP 54: 5°–40°C). It is made up of the following components:

Industrial Visual Display Terminal
With integrated 3.5" disk drive, printer output and lockable keyboard

Control Panel
Ergonomic design for easy access to the control buttons and LED display of input and output status

Teach Pendant
Protected with "deadmans" switch and emergency stop button

Serial Communication
Five available ports, including one for the supervisor link under DDCMP protocol, one for the ALTER protocol link for real time path control and three others for auxiliary functions

UNIT 18, Exercise 2

Let's go to a museum

Jane: Enjoy your breakfast?
Manfred: Yes, wonderful. Do you always have such a big breakfast?
Jane: Oh no, just on special occasions, you know – on Sundays sometimes, or when we have visitors. I just have a bit of muesli on normal weekdays.
Peter: So, what are we going to do? You still determined to see the Science Museum, Manfred?
Manfred: Yes, I'd like to see it very much.
Peter: Well, let's see then ... ah, we don't even have to change this time.
Jane: That's right, you just take the District Line all the way to South Kensington.
Manfred: Fine. That saves a lot of time.
Peter: OK, let's go then.

UNIT 19, Exercise 3

With computer-aided design and computer-aided manufacturing – CAD/CAM – the computer can keep track of all details, maintain design of parts in memory, and combine parts electronically as required.
Computer-aided design refers to the integration of computers and graphics-oriented software for the purpose of automating the design and drafting process. An engineer at a CAD site – often called an engineering workstation – can design a three-dimension part, analyze its characteristics, and then subject it to simulated stresses. If the part fails a stress test, its specifications can be changed at the workstation and it can then be retested. All these steps occur as the engineer works with the CAD hardware and software. Only after the engineer is satisfied that the part meets strength and other quality considerations are the design specifications released for production. Powerful CAD systems are now available for personal computers at a comparatively low cost. These PC-based CAD systems have greatly increased the number of professionals who design with computers, such as mechanical engineers, architects, landscape designers, technical illustrators, and artists. CAD systems offer a variety of advantages to graphic designers – designs are created quickly and can easily be modified. The designs are more precise, and can be used for cost and stress calculations; symbol libraries are used to help with future work. And designs can be stored in a data base to serve as a storehouse of knowledge for future designs.

Computer-aided manufacturing refers to the use of computers in the production process, and it is during this CAM phase that metal or other materials may first be machined to part specifications. The CAM process picks up where CAD leaves off – it provides a bridge between design and manufacturing. During the production phase, robots and other computer-controlled manufacturing tools are used to produce higher-quality products with more uniform tolerances than were previously feasible. As a manager at Chrysler said: "Many companies have design data and manufacturing data, and the two are never the same. At Chrysler, we have only one set of data that everyone uses."

UNIT 19, Exercise 6

<u>At the Science Museum (1)</u>

Peter: I don't think we can see everything in one day ...
Manfred: Probably not. Is this the hall where they have the old locomotives?
Peter: I think so – yes, over there, that's the Puffing Billy, built early in the nineteenth century.
Manfred: Fascinating.
Peter: They also have a special hall where they show a different exhibition every few months or so.
Manfred: Upstairs?
Peter: Probably.
Manfred: You know what they're showing at the moment?
Peter: Something to do with chemistry – ah yes, there's a poster – Chemical Industry – a kind of promotion, maybe, but quite interesting, I'm sure.

UNIT 20, Exercise 1

"I was flying over the valley and the lake. Below me a yellow sailing boat drifted on the river, and I saw a village along the water's edge. When I turned my head, green hills with fir trees stretched as far as the eye could see. I turned my head again, fixed my eyes on the little church and zoomed towards it. The door proved difficult to open, so I lifted the building and put it on my head in order to see inside."

Crazy? No, just virtual reality. A headset and a wired glove are all that's needed to transport you into a world of fantasy, a world where your dreams come true.
In the future, there will be more and more interaction of humans and computers. Instead of looking at a two-dimensional image on a screen as an outsider looking in, you become part of an artificial world of computer graphics in which you can walk around, move objects from one place to another, and even fly.
Inside the headset there are two pocket TVs with optics which give a wide-field view into the world of cyberspace or VR – virtual reality. An electro-magnetic system monitors the movements of the head so that the scene changes accordingly. The glove allows the sense of touch to be fed back to the person wearing it. Sometimes the glove is based on pneumatic air pockets which give a more realistic effect when objects are touched.

The possibilities are endless – in Japan, for instance, a virtual reality kitchen showroom enables housewives to put on a headset and build their ideal kitchen within the space of a small office. Housebuyers are able to have a look at new houses before they are built. Virtual reality is also used for training military pilots. There is a kind of super cockpit, which generates a virtual image of the scene, enabling the pilot to fly the aircraft without the dangers outside.

In the medical field, it is possible for surgeons to get inside a virtual reality world of, say, a patient's lung, and direct the radiation beams towards tumours with a much greater degree of accuracy.

Even language lessons could become a hobby rather than a headache. Virtual reality computer technology has the potential to transport pupils to the country of the language they are studying. Pupils learning French, for instance, could walk through the virtual reality streets of Paris where they would have the sense of wandering through shops and cafés and talking to people they meet in French.

Whatever it is used for, virtual reality gives users the 3-D look, sound and feel of an environment. Maybe some day the images will be so good that fantasy and reality become one.

UNIT 20, Exercise 3

At the Science Museum (2)

Manfred: Ah, I see – so this is the world's first steam engine, isn't it?
Peter: Not really. A lot of people think that James Watt invented the steam engine.
Manfred: I always thought so, too.
Peter: The very first steam engine is the one over there – it was designed by Thomas Newcomen, as a matter of fact.
Manfred: So he invented the steam engine?
Peter: Yes ... you see here ... in 1791.
Manfred: And the others are really just improvements.
Peter: Quite. New materials became available, you know – cast iron, for example, became a reliable material, and it was possible to use it for a lot of new things.

TESTING YOUR LANGUAGE – PART TWO

A. Listening comprehension

<u>What's going on with nuclear fusion?</u>

Stars make it look easy. They trap hydrogen at their core and press the colliding nuclei together until they fuse. This fusion releases energy – energy that makes the stars shine. Here on earth, one hi-tech substitute for the massiveness of stars is a room-size stainless-steel vacuum chamber at the Princeton Plasma Physics Laboratory. The chamber, which has the shape of a doughnut, is known as a tokamak. It is designed to hold plasma: gas heated to the point where the electrons in atoms are ripped out of their orbit, leaving a hot mass of nuclei and free electrons in the chamber. It is interesting to know that 99 percent of the visible matter in the universe is plasma.

When the tokamak is running, a thin cloud of plasma is pumped into the vacuum chamber every ten minutes. The plasma is then agitated with a pulsing voltage, which causes it to heat up. The plasma in the tokamak can reach temperatures of nearly 670 million degrees, 25 times hotter than the interior of the sun.

As the plasma temperature climbs, a 73,000-ampere electric current is sent through a series of 25-ton coils that are wrapped round the chamber. The current generates a magnetic field some 100,000 times stronger than Earth's. The magnetic field forms an invisible bottle that traps the plasma. During the few seconds the magnetic field can be sustained, the hot nuclei travel around the field inside the doughnut, reaching velocities of 3 million miles per hour. If the plasma is hot enough, dense enough, and confined enough, many of these speeding nuclei smash together and fuse.

The power to energize the coils comes from massive electrical generators next door. When current flows through the coils, there is a slight hum coming from the machine, and the hair of anyone right next to the generator stands on end.

Unfortunately, relatively little fusion takes place in the plasma. The reactor is not quite capable of simultaneously generating a high-enough temperature and sufficient magnetic force to achieve "scientific break-even": the point at which the fusion energy produced by the plasma equals the energy used to heat it. From there, it would still be a long way to "commercial break-even": the point when the cost of running a fusion reactor is low enough to make fusion competitive with other energy sources.

Compared with "dirty" energy sources, fusion is in many ways an environmentalist's dream. There is far less radioactive waste than with fission. Fusion does put out dangerous neutrons, but they can be stopped by shielding. Eventually the shielding and the walls of the fusion chamber become radioactive, but this radioacitivity is short-lived and relatively low-level. As important as these environmental issues are, there may be an even better reason to turn to fusion: we are running out of conventional fuels such as oil, gas and coal.

Based on an article in *Discover*

B. Listening comprehension

This is text one:

"If necessary, the centre column can be raised to a higher position. Rotate the locking collar to the right to unloosen and pull up he centre column to the desired height. Then rotate the locking collar to lock in place."

Now you're going to hear text two:

"Practical advice: If you wish, the ballhead can be unscrewed from the centre column and installed directly on the clamp housing."

This is the last text – text three:

"The clamp magic should be screwed on to the desired object (table, fence, chair leg, etc.). The clamp magic can open to a maximum of 3.4 inches (85 mm)."

Now decide which text goes into "B", "C" or "G".

Stichwortregister

accident report 68
algorithm 93
alignment 16
alumina trihydrate 35
aluminium 35, 37, 39, 41
applications 97
Armaturenbrett 13
artisan 8
auxiliary program 88
axis 80
Baustelle 47
bauxite 35
Bestandteile des Lehrwerks 4
Bewerbung 47, 48
Bewerbungsschreiben 52, 53
Brief 19
calibrate 59
car care 16, 17
caustic soda 35
chemical engineering 7
civil engineering 7
CNC 75
coating 57
controller 84
control systems 69
conveyors 33
craftsperson 8
cryolite 35
curriculum vitae 53
customize 93
CV 53
cybernetics 93
cyberspace 93
deadman's switch 84
dedicated 31
Dichtung 22
Diktat 5
drag 88
Edison, Thomas Alva 13
electrophoretic coating 31
engineering 8, 10
"English Plural"/"Foreign Plural" 55
ergonomics 84, 86

Fleming, Alexander 13
flowsheet 88
Flüssigkristallanzeige 27
Ford, Henry 13
galvatite 45
Grammatik 5
heat exchanger 84
hi-fi 71
Hörverständnis 5
incinerator 63
Ingenieurwesen 8
kommunikative Übungsformen 6
landfill 63
Lebenslauf 53
Leseverstehen 5
library 88
light rail transit 67
linear motor 18
liquid crystal display 27
logic chart 88
machine 75
machine tool safety 78
machining center 77
macro 93
maglev 20
mechanical engineering 7
Mehrzahl 55
menu-driven 93
metallurgy 7
mind 20
mineral fibre 22
Müllverbrennungsanlage 63
neoprene 22
network 91
note-taking 8, 27, 34, 56, 71
operating instructions 61
payload 80
port 84
Präpositionen 6
process engineering 7
pull-down menu 88
quite 46
radiator 22

Realien 6
Regler 80
resin 63
resumé 53
robot 82
ruggedize 94
scale 88
schriftliche Arbeit 6
Schweißen 43
servomechanism 80
site 47
solar energy 24
sophisticated 75
spark plug 71
spreadsheet 94
Stellenanzeige 52
symbol table 88

Technik 8
technique 8
Technologie 8
telecommunications 7
telephone 96
thermocouple 59
tile 71
titanium 35
tune 71
Tuning 71
Unfallbericht 68
virtual reality 97
Wärmetauscher 84
welding 43
Wortschatz 6
yarn 65